CLASSICS IN PSYCHOLOGY

CLASSICS IN PSYCHOLOGY

A NOTE ABOUT THE AUTHOR

JACQUES LOEB was born in Mayen, Germany, in 1859. He studied in Berlin and Munich and received his M. D. from Strasbourg in 1884. After conducting research in Naples for several years, he emigrated to the United States in 1891. He taught at Bryn Mawr, Chicago and Berlin before becoming a member of the Rockefeller Institute for Medical Research in 1910.

As a pioneer in experimental biology, Loeb was most famous for his work in artificial parthenogenesis. He developed larvae of sea urchins from unfertilized eggs and later raised parthenogenetic frogs to sexual maturity. Loeb also did important work on the physiology of the brain, regeneration, and the nature of life processes; throughout his writings he attempted to explain mental processes in terms of fundamental tropisms. Loeb died in 1924.

Comparative Physiology of the Brain and Comparative Psychology

By

Jacques Loeb, M.D.

orig 1900

ARNO PRESS
A New York Times Company
New York ★ 1973

Reprint Edition 1973 by Arno Press Inc.

Reprinted from a copy in
The University of Illinois Library

Classics in Psychology
ISBN for complete set: 0-405-05130-1
See last pages of this volume for titles.

Manufactured in the United *States of America

————◆————

Library of Congress Cataloging in Publication Data

Loeb, Jacques, 1859-1924.
  Comparative physiology of the brain and comparative
psychology.

  (Classics in psychology)
  Reprint of the ed. published by Putnam, New York, in
the Science series.
  Translation of Einleitung in die vergleichende
gehirnphysiologie.
  Includes bibliographies.
  1. Brain. 2. Psychology, Comparative. I. Title.
[DNLM: WL L825e 1900F]
QP376.L6213 1973   591.1'88   72-2973
ISBN 0-405-05146-8

The Science Series

EDITED BY

Professor J. McKeen Cattell, M.A., Ph.D.

AND

F. E. Beddard, M.A., F.R.S.

COMPARATIVE PHYSIOLOGY OF THE BRAIN AND COMPARATIVE PSYCHOLOGY

Comparative Physiology of the Brain and Comparative Psychology

By

Jacques Loeb, M.D.

Professor of Physiology in the University of Chicago

Illustrated

New York

G. P. Putnam's Sons

London: John Murray

1900

The Knickerbocker Press, New York

PREFACE

It is the purpose of this book to serve as a short introduction to the comparative physiology of the brain and of the central nervous system.

Physiology has thus far been essentially the physiology of Vertebrates. I am convinced, however, that for the establishment of the laws of life-phenomena a broader basis is necessary. Such a basis can be furnished only by a comparative physiology which includes all classes of the animal kingdom. My experience in the course on comparative physiology at Wood's Holl seems to indicate that the transition from the old to the comparative physiology can be most readily accomplished through the physiology of the central nervous system.

The physiology of the brain has been rendered unnecessarily difficult through the fact that metaphysicians have at all times concerned themselves with the interpretation of brain functions and have introduced such metaphysical conceptions as soul, consciousness, will, etc. One part of the work of the physiologist must consist in the substitution of *real* physiological processes for these inadequate conceptions. Professor Ernst Mach, of Vienna, to whom

v

this book is dedicated, was the first to establish the general principles of an antimetaphysical science.

I have added at the end of each chapter a list of the chief papers of which I have made use. Although far from complete, this may serve the beginner as a guide for the further study of the subjects touched upon.

The book appeared first in German and was translated by Anne Leonard Loeb. As a number of new facts have been found since the German edition appeared, and as it seemed desirable to formulate my antimetaphysical standpoint more precisely, I have made extensive alterations.

My thanks are due to a number of friends who have offered suggestions,—most of all to my pupil, Miss Anne Moore.

THE UNIVERSITY OF CHICAGO,
October 1, 1900.

CONTENTS

vii

ILLUSTRATIONS IN THE TEXT

ix

COMPARATIVE PHYSIOLOGY OF THE BRAIN
AND COMPARATIVE PSYCHOLOGY

INTRODUCTION TO

THE COMPARATIVE PHYSIOLOGY OF THE BRAIN

CHAPTER I

SOME FUNDAMENTAL FACTS AND CONCEPTIONS CONCERNING THE COMPARATIVE PHYSIOLOGY OF THE CENTRAL NERVOUS SYSTEM

1. The understanding of complicated phenomena depends upon an analysis by which they are resolved into their simple elementary components. If we ask what the elementary components are in the physiology of the central nervous system, our attention is directed to a class of processes which are called reflexes. A reflex is a reaction which is caused by an external stimulus, and which results in a coördinated movement, the closing of the eyelid, for example, when the conjunctiva is touched by a foreign body, or the narrowing of the pupil under the influence of light. In each of these cases, changes in the sensory

nerve-endings are produced which bring about a change of condition in the nerves. This change travels to the central nervous system, passes from there to the motor nerves, and terminates in the muscle-fibres, producing there a contraction. This passage from the stimulated part to the central nervous system, and back again to the peripheral muscles, is called a reflex. There has been a growing tendency in physiology to make reflexes the basis of the analysis of the functions of the central nervous system, consequently much importance has been attached to the underlying processes and the necessary mechanisms.

The name reflex suggests a comparison between the spinal cord and a mirror. Sensory stimuli were supposed to be reflected from the spinal cord to the muscles; destruction of the spinal cord would, according to this, make the reflex impossible, just as the breaking of the mirror prevents the reflection of light. This comparison, however, of the reflex process in the central nervous system with the reflection of light has, long since, become meaningless, and at present few physiologists in using the term reflex think of its original significance. Instead of this, another feature in the conception of the term reflex has gained prominence, namely, the *purposeful* character of many reflex movements. The closing of the eyelid and the narrowing of the pupil are eminently purposeful, for the cornea is protected from hurtful contact with foreign bodies, and the retina from the injurious effects of strong light. Another striking characteristic in such reflexes has also been emphasised. The movements which are produced are so well planned and coördinated that it seems as though some intelligence were at work either in devising or in carrying them out. The fact, however, that a decapitated frog will brush a drop of acetic acid from its skin, suggests that some other explanation is necessary. A prominent psychologist has maintained that reflexes are to be considered as the mechanical effects of acts of volition of past generations. The ganglion-cell seems the only place where such mechanical effects could be stored up. It has therefore been considered the most essential element of the reflex mechanism, the nerve-fibres being regarded, and probably correctly, merely as conductors.

Both the authors who emphasise the purposefulness of the reflex act, and those who see in it only a physical process, have invariably looked upon the ganglion-cell as the principal bearer of the structures for the complex coördinated movements in reflex action.

I should have been as little inclined as any other physiologist to doubt the correctness of this conception had not the establishment of the identity of the reactions of animals and plants to light proved the untenability of this view and at the same time offered a different conception of reflexes. The flight of the moth into the flame is a typical reflex process. The light stimulates the peripheral sense organs, the stimulus passes to the central nervous system, and from there to the muscles of the wings, and the moth is caused to fly into the flame. This reflex process agrees in every point with the heliotropic effects of light on plant organs. Since plants possess no nerves, this identity of animal with plant heliotropism can offer but one inference — these heliotropic effects must depend upon conditions which are common to both animals and plants. At the end of my book on heliotropism I expressed this view in the following words : "We have seen that, in the case of animals which possess nerves, the movements of orientation toward light are governed by exactly the same external conditions, and depend in the same way upon the external form of the body, as in the case of plants which possess no nerves. These heliotropic phenomena, consequently, cannot depend upon *specific* qualities of the central nervous system (1)." On the other hand, the objection has been raised that destruction of the ganglion-cells interrupts the reflex process. This argument, however, is not sound, for the nervous reflex arc in higher animals forms the only protoplasmic bridge between the sensory organs of the surface of the body and the muscles. If we destroy the ganglion-cells or the central nervous system, we interrupt the continuity of the protoplasmic conduction between the surface of the body and the muscles, and a reflex is no longer possible. Since the axis-cylinders of the nerves and the ganglion-cells are nothing more than protoplasmic formations, we are justified in seeking in them only general protoplasmic qualities, unless we find that the phenomena cannot be explained by means of the latter alone.

2. A further objection has been raised, that although these reflexes occur in plants possessing no nervous system, yet in animals where ganglion-cells are present the very existence of ganglion-cells necessitates the presence in them of special reflex mechanisms. It was therefore necessary to find out if there were not animals in which coördinated reflexes still continued to exist after the destruction of the central nervous system. Such a phenomenon could be expected only in forms in which a direct transmission of stimuli from the skin to the muscle is possible, in addition to the transmission through the reflex arc. This is the case, for instance, in worms and in Ascidians. I succeeded in demonstrating in *Ciona intestinalis* that the complicated reflexes still continue after removal of the central nervous system (2).

A study, then, of comparative physiology brings out the fact that irritability and conductibility are the only qualities essential to reflexes, and these are both common qualities of all protoplasm. The irritable structures at the surface of the body, and the arrangement of the muscles, determine the character of the reflex act. The assumption that the central nervous system or the ganglion-cells are the bearers of reflex mechanisms cannot hold. But have we now to conclude that the nerves are superfluous and a waste? Certainly not. Their value lies in the fact that they are quicker and more sensitive conductors than undifferentiated protoplasm. Because of these qualities of the nerves, an animal is better able to adapt itself to changing conditions than it possibly could if it had no nerves. Such power of adaptation is absolutely necessary for free animals.

3. While some authors explain all reflexes on a psychical basis, the majority of investigators explain in this way only a certain group of reflexes — the so-called instincts. Instincts are defined in various ways, but no matter how the definition is phrased the meaning seems to be that they are inherited reflexes so purposeful and so complicated in character that nothing short of intelligence and experience could have produced them. To this class of reflexes belongs the habit possessed by certain insects of laying their eggs on the material which the larvæ will afterwards require for food. When we consider that the female fly pays no attention to her eggs after laying them, we cannot cease to wonder at the seeming care which nature takes for the preservation of the species. How can the action of such an insect be determined if not by mysterious structures which can only be contained in the ganglion-cells? How can we explain the inheritance of such instincts if we believe it to be a fact that the ganglion-cells are only the conductors of stimuli? It was impossible either to develop a mechanics of instincts or to explain their inheritance in a simple way from the old standpoint, but our conception makes an explanation possible. Among the

elements which compose these complicated instincts, the tropisms (heliotropism, chemotropism, geotropism, stereotropism) play an important part. These tropisms are identical for animals and plants. The explanation of them depends first upon the specific irritability of certain elements of the body-surface, and, second, upon the relations of symmetry of the body. Symmetrical elements at the surface of the body have the same irritability; unsymmetrical elements have a different irritability. Those nearer the oral pole possess an irritability greater than that of those near the aboral pole. These circumstances force an animal to orient itself toward a source of stimulation in such a way that symmetrical points on the surface of the body are stimulated equally. In this way the animals are led without will of their own either toward the source of the stimulus or away from it. Thus there remains nothing for the ganglion-cell to do but to conduct the stimulus, and this may be accomplished by protoplasm in any form. For the inheritance of instincts it is only necessary that the egg contain certain substances — which will determine the different tropisms — and the conditions for producing bilateral symmetry of the embryo. The mystery with which the ganglion-cell has been surrounded has led not only to no definite insight into these processes, but has proved rather a hindrance in the attempt to find the explanation of them.

It is evident that there is no sharp line of demarcation between reflexes and instincts. We find that authors prefer to speak of reflexes in cases where the reaction of single parts or organs of an animal to external stimuli is concerned ; while they speak of instincts where the reaction of the animal as a whole is involved (as is the case in tropisms).

4. If the mechanics of a number of instincts is explained by means of the tropisms common to animals and plants, and if the significance of the ganglion-cells is confined, as in all reflex processes, to their power of conducting stimuli, we are forced to ask what circumstances determine the coördinated movements in reflexes, especially in the more complicated ones. The assumption of complicated but unknown and perhaps unknowable structures in the ganglion-cells served formerly as a convenient terminus for all thought in this direction. In giving up this assumption, we are called upon to show what conditions are able to determine the coördinated character of reflex movements. Experiments on galvanotropism of animals have proved that a simple relation must exist between the orientation of certain motor elements in the central nervous system and the direction of the movements of the body which is called forth by the activity of these elements. This perhaps creates a rational basis for the further investigation of coördinated movements.

5. We must also deprive the ganglion-cells of all specific significance in spontaneous movements, just as we have done in the case of simple reflexes and instincts. By spontaneous movements we mean

movements which are apparently determined by internal conditions of the living system. Strictly speaking, no movements of animals are exclusively determined by internal conditions, for the atmospheric oxygen and a certain temperature or certain limits of temperature are always necessary in order to preserve the activity beyond a short period of time.

We must discriminate between simple and conscious spontaneity. In simple spontaneity we must consider two kinds of processes, namely, aperiodic spontaneous processes and rhythmically spontaneous or automatic processes. The rhythmical processes are of importance for our consideration. Respiration and the heart-beat belong to this category. The respiratory movements prove without possible doubt that automatic activity *can* arise in the ganglion-cells, and from this the conclusion has been drawn that all automatic movements are due to specific structures of the ganglion-cells. Recent investigations, however, have transferred the problem of rhythmical spontaneous contractions from the field of morphology into that of physical chemistry. The peculiar qualities of each tissue are partly due to the fact that it contains ions (Na, K, Ca, and others) in definite proportions. By changing these proportions, we can impart to a tissue properties which it does not ordinarily possess. If in the muscles of the skeleton the Na ions be increased and the Ca ions be reduced, the muscles are able to contract rhythmically, like the heart. It is only the presence of Ca ions in the blood which prevents the muscles of our skeleton from beating rhythmically in our body. As the muscles contain no ganglion-cells, it is certain that the power of rhythmical spontaneous contractions is not due to the specific morphological character of the ganglion-cells, but to definite chemical conditions which are not necessarily confined to ganglion-cells (3).

The coördinated character of automatic movements has often been explained by a " centre of coördination," which is supposed to keep a kind of police watch on the different elements and see that they move in the right order. Observations in lower animals, however, show that the coördination of automatic movements is caused by the fact that that element which beats most quickly forces the others to beat in its own rhythm. Aperiodic spontaneity is still less a specific function of the ganglion-cell than rhythmical spontaneity. The swarm-spores of algæ, which possess no ganglion-cells, show spontaneity equal to that of animals having ganglion-cells.

6. Thus far we have not touched upon the most important problem in physiology, namely, which mechanisms give rise to that complex of phenomena which are called psychic or conscious. Our method of procedure must be the same as in the case of instincts and reflexes. We must find out the elementary physiological processes which underlie the complicated phenomena of consciousness. Some

physiologists and psychologists consider the purposefulness of the psychic action as the essential element. If an animal or an organ reacts as a rational man would do under the same circumstances, these authors declare that we are dealing with a phenomenon of consciousness. In this way many reflexes, the instincts especially, are looked upon as psychic functions. Consciousness has been ascribed even to the spinal cord, because many of its functions are purposeful. We shall see in the following chapters that many of these reactions are merely tropisms which may occur in exactly the same form in plants. Plants must therefore have a psychic life, and, following the argument, we must ascribe it to machines also, for the tropisms depend only on simple mechanical arrangements. In the last analysis, then, we would arrive at molecules and atoms endowed with mental qualities.

We can dispose of this view by the mere fact that the phenomena of embryological development and of organisation in general show a degree of purposefulness which may even surpass that of any reflex or instinctive or conscious act. And yet we do not consider the phenomena of development to be dependent upon consciousness.

On the other hand, physiologists who have appreciated the untenable character of such metaphysical speculations have held that the only alternative is to drop the search for the mechanisms underlying consciousness and study exclusively the results of operations on the brain. This would be throwing out the wheat with the chaff. The mistake made by metaphysicians is not that they devote themselves to fundamental problems, but that they employ the wrong methods of investigation and substitute a play on words for explanation by means of facts. If brain-physiology gives up its fundamental problem, namely, the discovery of those elementary processes which make consciousness possible, it abandons its best possibilities. But to obtain results, the errors of the metaphysician must be avoided and explanations must rest upon facts, not words. The method should be the same for animal psychology that it is for brain-physiology. It should consist in the right understanding of the fundamental process which recurs in all psychic phenomena as the elemental component. *This process, according to my opinion, is the activity of the associative memory, or of association.* Consciousness is only a metaphysical term for phenomena which are determined by associative memory. By associative memory I mean that mechanism by which a stimulus brings about not only the effects which its nature and the specific structure of the irritable organ call for, but by which it brings about also the effects of other stimuli which formerly acted upon the organism almost or quite simultaneously with the stimulus in question (4). If an animal can be trained, if it can learn, it possesses associative memory. By means of this criterion it can be shown that Infusoria, Cœlenterates, and worms do not possess a trace of associative memory. Among certain classes of insects (for instance, wasps), the existence of associative memory can be proved. It is a comparatively easy task to find out which representatives of the various classes of animals possess, and which do not possess, associative memory. Our criterion therefore might be of great assistance in the development of comparative psychology.

7. Our criterion puts an end to the metaphysical ideas that all matter, and hence the whole animal world, possesses consciousness. We are brought to the theory that only certain species of animals possess associative memory and have consciousness, and that it appears in them only after they have reached a certain stage in their ontogenetic development. This is apparent from the fact that associative memory depends upon mechanical arrangements which are present only in certain animals, and present in these only after a certain development has been reached. The fact that certain vertebrates lose all power of associative memory after the destruction of the cerebral hemispheres, and the fact that vertebrates in which the associative memory either is not developed at all or only slightly developed (*e. g.*, the shark or frog) do not differ, or differ but slightly, in their reactions after losing the cerebral hemispheres, support this view. The fact that only certain animals possess the necessary

mechanical arrangements for associative memory, and therefore for metaphysical consciousness, is not stranger than the fact that only certain animals possess the mechanical arrangements for uniting the rays from a luminous point in one point on the retina. The liquefaction of gases is an example of a sudden change of condition which may be produced when one variable is changed ; it is not surprising that there should be sudden changes in the ontogenetic and phylogenetic development of organisms when there are so many variables subject to change, and when we consider that colloids easily change their state of matter.

It becomes evident that the unravelling of the mechanism of associative memory is the great discovery to be made in the field of brain-physiology and psychology. But at the same time it is evident that this mechanism cannot be unravelled by histological methods, or by operations on the brain, or by measuring reaction times. We have to remember that all life phenomena are ultimately due to motions or changes occurring in colloidal substances. The question is, Which peculiarities of the colloidal substances can make the phenomenon of associative memory possible ? For the solution of this problem the experience of physical chemistry and of the physiology of the protoplasm must be combined. From the same sources we must expect the solution of the other fundamental problems of brain-physiology, namely, the process of conduction of stimuli.

BIBLIOGRAPHY.

1. LOEB, J. *Der Heliotropismus der Thiere und seine Ueberein-stimmung mit dem Heliotropismus der Pflanzen.* Würzburg, 1890. A preliminary note on these experiments appeared January, 1888.

2. LOEB, J. *Untersuchungen zur physiologischen Morphologie der Thiere II.* Würzburg, 1892.

3. LOEB, J. *American Journal of Physiology*, vol. iii., p. 327 and p. 383, 1900.

4. LOEB, J. *Beiträge zur Gehirnphysiologie der Würmer. Pflüger's Archiv*, Band lvi., 1894.

CHAPTER II

THE CENTRAL NERVOUS SYSTEM OF MEDUSAE.
EXPERIMENTS ON SPONTANEITY AND CO-
ORDINATION

1. Experiments on Medusæ or jelly-fish afford us an excellent opportunity for analysing the conditions for spontaneity and coördination, and for deciding whether or not these phenomena are dependent upon ganglion-cells. The subumbrella of the Medusæ has a very thin layer of muscle-fibres which contract rhythmically. The contraction diminishes the size of the swimming-bell, and forces the water out. By means of the recoil the animal moves forward. In regard to the nervous system, we must discriminate between two classes of Medusæ : first, the Hydromedusæ (Hydroidea, Fig. 1), and, second, the Acalephæ, one representative of which (*Aurelia aurita*, Fig. 2) is familiar to many laymen. The nervous system of the Hydromedusæ consists of a double nerve-ring along the margin of the umbrella (*d*, Fig. 1). The upper nerve-ring forms a flat layer in the ectoderm, and consists of thin fibres and ganglion-cells. The lower nerve-ring has thicker fibres

and more ganglion-cells, and is connected with the upper ring by nerve-fibres. In addition to this ring, which is called the central nervous system, there is also a peripheral nervous system, a plexus, consisting of nerves and scattered ganglion cells, spread out over the whole subumbrella (*b*, Fig. 1), between the epithelium and the muscle-layer. The convex surface of the umbrella consists of a non-contractile, gelatinous mass, and no nervous elements are to be found in it.

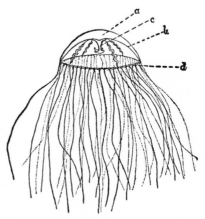

FIG. 1. HYDROMEDUSA. (Gonionemus vertens.)

a, umbrella ; *b*, subumbrella with muscles ; *c*, manubrium ; *d*, margin of the swimming-bell with the nerve-ring.

Acalephæ (Fig. 2) have no continuous nerve-ring, but a row of separate nerve-centres (*S*, Fig. 2) extends around the margin of the umbrella, lying in the ectoderm, which covers the basis of the marginal bodies (sense organs). The number of these centres corresponds, at least in *Aurelia aurita*, with the number of sense organs. This nervous system contains no ganglion-cells, but processes called nerve-fibres go out from special epithelial cells. The muscle-layer of the umbrella also is said to contain a peripheral nervous plexus (1).

2

Our first question is : Is the spontaneous locomotion of the Medusæ, or the rhythmical contraction of their swimming-bell, a function of the ganglion-cells ?

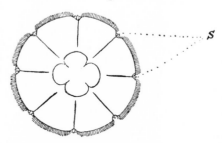

FIG. 2. DIAGRAM OF THE BELL OF AURELIA AURITA, WITH EIGHT SENSE ORGANS. (After Claus.)

Romanes found that if the margin of the bell of a Hydromedusa (*b*, Fig. 3) be cut off, the rhythmical contraction of the centre of the bell (*a*, Fig. 3) ceases, while the margin *b*, which contains the nerve-ring, continues to execute rhythmical contractions (2). The wound does not even cause a decrease in the number or in the strength of the marginal contractions. The experiment has been repeated by other authors with the same result. Any sort of wound can be made in the umbrella without disturbing the rhythmical contractions so long as the nerve-ring remains intact. Thus Romanes concluded that these rhythmical contractions of Hydromedusæ originate in the nerve-ring or its ganglia. I have found recently that this whole problem is not so much a morphological problem as a problem of physical chemistry. The osmotic pressure of the sea-water is about equal to that of a $\frac{5}{8}$ n NaCl solution. I found that if the centre of a swimming-bell be put into a $\frac{5}{8}$ n NaCl or $\frac{5}{8}$ n NaBr solution it goes on beating rhythmically. But if a small quantity of $CaCl_2$ or KCl, or both, be added, the centre stops beating. The centre would beat in sea-water were it not for the presence there of Ca, K, and possibly other ions (3). The centre contains some scattered ganglion-cells. It might be argued that the presence of these cells makes the rhythmical contractions in a pure NaCl solution possible. It is easy to prove that such is not the case. The striped skeletal muscles of a frog do not contract rhythmically in blood or serum. I have shown that this is due to the presence of Ca ions in these liquids.

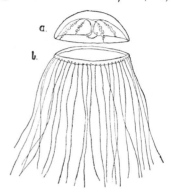

FIG. 3. EXPERIMENT IN DIVIDING A HYDROMEDUSA.

The amputated margin continues to contract rhythmically, while the bell no longer contracts.

If the muscle be put into a pure NaCl or NaBr solution of the same osmotic pressure as the blood, the muscles contract rhythmically (4). Yet these muscles contain no ganglion-cells. *Hence it is not the presence or absence of ganglion-cells which determines the spontaneous rhythmical contractions, but the presence or absence of certain ions. Na ions start or increase the rate of spontaneous rhythmical contractions ; Ca ions diminish the rate or inhibit such contractions altogether.* How can these ions have such an influence? In order to explain this we must go back to the fundamental character of protoplasmic motion. Protoplasmic motions are due to changes in the physical character of the colloidal material in the protoplasm. These changes may consist in changes in the state of matter or in the absorption of water by these colloids, or in secondary changes derived from those before mentioned. We know that the physical qualities of the colloids are influenced greatly by the nature and osmotic pressure of the ions in the surrounding solution. For that labile equilibrium of the colloids which is required for spontaneous rhythmical contractions, the Na, Ca, and K ions must be present in definite proportions in the tissues. This proportion must be different for the centre and the margin of a Hydromedusa. While for the margin the proportion in which these three ions exist in the sea-water is adequate, for the centre of a Hydromedusa more Na ions and less Ca ions are required. Hence, if we put a centre without the margin into normal sea-water it does not beat, but it will beat when put into a pure NaCl or NaBr solution of the same osmotic pressure as sea-water. In the pure NaCl solution Na ions of the solution will enter into the tissues and take the place of some of the Ca ions. This will give the colloids of the muscles those qualities which allow rhythmical contractions. If too many Na ions enter the tissues of the centre it will lose its irritability. The latter will, in this case, be restored again by adding a trace of $CaCl_2$ to the solution. It thus happens that the problem of spontaneous activity is no longer a question of the presence or absence of the ganglion-

cells, but of the physical qualities of the colloidal substances in the tissues. But must we conclude from
this that the Na ions are the cause of the spontaneous
rhythmical contractions of the Medusæ? I think
not. The ions only bring about a certain labile equi-

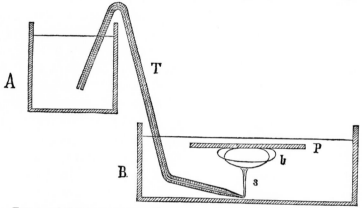

Fig. 4. Arrangement for Producing Automatically Pulsating
Air-Bubbles. (See text.)

librium in the condition of the colloids of the contractile tissue which allows the true cause of the
contractions to be effective. But what is this
cause?

J. Rosenthal seems to have been the first to call
attention to the fact that it is in no way essential for
a rhythmical phenomenon to have a rhythmical cause,
and that constant conditions can lead to rhythmical
effects. If a small, constant stream of water flows
into a pipette, it will pass out rhythmically in drops.
The weight of the drop must be greater than the

surface-tension in the periphery of the opening of the outlet before the drop can break off. As long as the quantity of water running into the pipette, in the unit of time, remains below a certain limit, it will be some time before the drop will be heavy enough to fall. Quincke has given a simple and elegant method by which it is easy to produce *rhythmical contractions* in air bubbles (5). I will describe the experiment as shown in my lectures. A glass plate P (Fig. 4) is placed in a dish B, filled with water. The lower, narrow end of the thermometer tube T is under and at the middle of the air-bubble, while the upper end rests in a dish A filled with 95 per cent. alcohol. The alcohol rises in a fine stream toward the centre of the bubble. As soon as the alcohol comes in contact with the bubble, the alcohol spreads out on the limit between the air and the water, because the sum of the surface-tensions between air and alcohol and alcohol and water is less than the surface-tension between air and water. By the decrease in the surface-tension the bubble becomes flatter and broader. In consequence of the vortex movements in the water that are produced by the spreading, the flow of the alcohol to the bubble is interrupted. The layer of alcohol around the bubble diffuses rapidly into the surrounding water, and the bubble becomes again higher and narrower. The alcohol can flow to the bubble again now that the vortex-movements have ceased, and the flattening of the bubble again takes place, and so on. Under the above-mentioned conditions I obtained about eighty pulsations per minute — *i. e.*, about the periodicity of the heart.

Now, as regards the origin of the rhythmical activity of Medusæ, of the heart, and of respiratory activity, we can imagine that a constant fermentative production of certain compounds in the automatically active cell corresponds to the constant flow of alcohol in Quincke's experiment. These substances may be of such a nature that they occasion spreading-phenomena or some other physical change in the colloids of the muscle. But a certain quantity of these substances must be present before this change occurs, hence the periodicity of the contractions. But whether it be a constant fermentative production of some substance or not, the ultimate constant cause for the production is the heat or the intensity factor of the same — the temperature. It now can no longer surprise us that Romanes found that the centre of an Acalepha is able to beat rhythmically in normal sea-water if severed from the margin. As long as we assume that the ganglion-cells are the essential element in spontaneity, this experience on Acalephæ would be difficult to explain. As it is, we are only obliged to conclude that in Acalephæ there is less difference between the colloidal substances of the margin and centre than in Hydromedusæ.

2.   Not only the spontaneous character of locomotions is commonly considered to be due to ganglion-cells, but the coördinated character of these motions as well. Let us see how far this notion is correct.

Romanes found that if the whole margin of the umbrella of a Hydromedusa be cut off, and only a tiny piece left, this is sufficient to keep up the spontaneous activity of the jelly-fish in sea-water. From this it would appear that any element of the margin may be considered a centre for the rhythmical contractions of the whole Medusa. But if this be the case, how does it happen that the whole umbrella contracts simultaneously, and why do we not find one part of the margin in systole and the other in diastole? This coördination is by no means to be taken for granted. It is present only in healthy specimens, and is wanting in injured or dying specimens, a fact to which Romanes called attention. The problem of the mechanism of this coördination has been dismissed by many authors by the assumption of a "coördinating centre" that is supposed to control this coördination. We shall shortly be in a position to decide whether coördination in lower animals is controlled by a special "centre of coördination," or whether it is not rather the result of simple laws of stimulation and conduction.

Romanes found in Acalephæ that coördination ceases when all direct connection between the nervous centres has been interrupted by radial incisions in the umbrella, the various sectors no longer contracting simultaneously. The same thing results in Hydromedusæ, if conduction through the nerve-ring is interrupted. In such cases, the radial incision must reach well toward the centre of the bell. If, however, such incisions are made in the umbrella without injuring the margin and the nerve-ring, no disturbance of coördination ensues. It seems that the continuity of the structures located in the marginal portions of the umbrella is necessary for the coördinated activity. Now how does it happen that so long as the continuity is preserved all the elements act synchronically, while the synchronism disappears if the continuity is interrupted?[1] In order to answer this question, we must turn our attention to an organ which shows the phenomena of coördinated rhythmical activity in a striking manner—namely, the heart. If the heart of a frog be divided into several pieces, they will all be rhythmically active, but the *number* of contractions will vary in the different pieces. The sinus venosus beats most rapidly, and the number of its contractions in a unit of time equals that of the heart before it was divided. *Thus we see that the whole heart beats in the rhythm of the part that has the maximum number of contractions per minute. From this we must assume that the coördination of the heart's activity is due to the fact that the part which contracts most frequently, forces the other parts to contract in the same rhythm.* They will be forced to do this if the activity of the sinus venosus acts as a stimulus upon the other parts. A centre of coördination is therefore entirely unnecessary.

Porter succeeded by an ingenious method in causing

[1] It should be emphasised that incisions through the margin alone do not interfere with coördination in Gonionemus, but that it is necessary to continue the incisions to the centre of the swimming-bell. But even under such circumstances the animal may still contract in a coördinated way.

strips of a mammalian heart to beat. He also draws from his observations the conclusion that there is no reason for assuming the existence of a centre of a coördination (6). In Medusæ, also, a synchronical contraction of all the parts takes place if the stimulus from the portion first active can travel rapidly enough to the rest of the margin. This is only possible when the margin is uninjured. It is evident, however, that the neighbouring tissue as well as the nerve-ring is involved, because the radial incision must reach well toward the centre of the bell if we wish to stop the coördination. In this case the wave of stimulation must pass around the incisions, a process which involves so much time that the separate parts are able to contract independently, and the synchronism is lost. In injured or dying Medusæ, where the contact of the cells is less close, uncoördinated, rhythmical activity occurs.

In order to test this idea further, I proposed to Dr. Hargitt, who was working in my laboratory, that he attempt to graft two Hydromedusæ, and observe whether they continue to contract synchronically or independently after healing. For this purpose it was necessary to remove the margin of the Medusæ. Two of them were then placed with their wounded surfaces in contact, and kept in this position. Figure 5 shows two Gonionemi grafted in this way. They grew together along the entire line of contact with the exception of a small part at *O*. New tentacles would probably have developed there in time had we not killed the animals in order to preserve them. In other experiments, the two animals did not heal together so completely. It happened in the case where the animals had grown together most completely, as represented in Figure 5, that they contracted synchronically like one animal two days after the operation. The animals, on the other hand, that had not grown together to such an extent did not contract synchronically. I believe that if one could succeed in healing two hearts together completely, they would also beat synchronically.

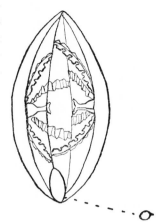

FIG. 5. DR. HARGITT'S EXPERIMENT.

Two Gonionemi grafted together. Two days after the operation synchronous contractions of both animals were observed.

The assumption of a "centre of coördination" situated in the ganglia of the margin of a Medusa thus becomes unnecessary. In the frog's heart, the sinus venosus beats faster than the auricle, ventricle, and bulbus aortæ. Hence, each contraction of the sinus venosus acts as a stimulus, which causes a contraction of the auricles, and the contraction of the latter is the stimulus which causes the contraction of the ventricle and bulbus aortæ. It would follow from this that if we could cause the bulbus aortæ in the frog's heart to beat as fast as the sinus venosus we might see a reversal of the heart-beat. Nature has made this experiment for us on a large scale in the Ascidian's heart (Fig. 6).

The latter has the peculiarity that the waves of contraction do not spread out con-

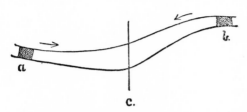

FIG. 6.   DIAGRAM OF THE ASCIDIAN HEART.

In the Ascidian heart, contractions occur for a time in the direction from *a* to *b*, and then from *b* to *a*. If the heart be cut open at *c*, the left half contracts only in the direction from *a* to *c*, the right half only in the direction from *b* to *c*.

stantly in one direction, as in the hearts of other animals, but peristaltic and antiperistaltic waves of contraction alternate in it. If, for example, it has contracted five hundred times in succession from left to right, sending the blood to the right, this activity is followed by perhaps three hundred pulsations from right to left, which cause the blood to flow through the blood-vessels in the opposite direction. These contractions are followed again by a large number of pulsations from left to right, etc. Mr. Lingle made the following experiments on the Ascidian's heart at Wood's Holl in 1892. If *a b* (Fig. 6) be an Ascidian's heart and it be divided at *c*, both pieces, *a c*, and *b c*, contract uninterruptedly in a constant direction, the former in the direction from *a* to *c*, and the latter in the direction from *b* to *c*. Mr. Lingle found, furthermore, that the source of the automatic activity is confined to two small regions (*a* and *b*, Fig. 6) which correspond to the sinus venosus and the bulbus aortæ of the frog's heart. When we excise these two pieces from the heart they continue to beat without interruption, while the long part between the two pieces no longer pulsates (in sea-water at least). These experiments, it seems to me, leave no room for doubt that the change in the direction of the contraction in the Ascidian's heart is determined by each of the two ends getting the upper hand alternately, and forcing the other centre to act in its rhythm for a time. This "getting the upper hand" might possibly mean nothing more than that one end gains the time in which to send off a wave of contraction before the other end begins to contract. For this it is only necessary that a single heart-beat of the leading end be delayed or fail entirely, a phenomenon that also appears occasionally in the human heart. In this way the other end of the heart gains time in which to send out a wave of contraction, and its automatic activity will continue to be the stimulus for the activity of the first end until a delay occurs in one beat or until one beat is skipped, thus allowing the first end time again to become automatically active, and so on.

Last year I asked the members of the class in general physiology at Wood's Holl to find out whether the latter view was correct. Their observations were as follows : Suppose at a certain time *a* to be the active and *b* the passive end of the heart. After a short time *a* begins to beat more slowly or ceases to beat altogether. During the pause, the end *b* succeeds in sending out a wave of contraction which reaches *a* before it has had time to send out a wave of its own. One sees occasionally at the time of a reversal that at first both ends send out contraction-waves which may meet in the middle of the heart. At the next heart-beat, the end which is about to stop delays the sending out of the wave a little more, and at the next heart-beat the wave starting from the other end can pass over the whole heart without being blocked.

Hence the coördination of movements in Medusæ (or in the heart) is not due to a hypothetical centre of coördination situated in the ganglion-cells, but to the fact that the element which is first active acts as a stimulus upon its next element, and so on.

3. It may be shown that even more specialised forms of coördination do not depend upon the presence or interference of ganglia. When the back of a frog is touched with acetic acid, the frog wipes off the acid with its foot. If one leg is tied, it uses the other for this purpose. The turtle acts in a similar manner when acetic acid is applied to the back of its shell. It cannot reach the stimulated spot, but the legs move dorsally under the shell as far as possible towards it. Physiology has contented itself in regard to these phenomena by pointing to the complicated nature and impenetrable structural secrets of the central nervous system. Yet the same reactions occur in a Hydromedusa, in which case the term

"central nervous system" has only a conventional significance. Romanes found that if we stimulate a spot *a* (Fig. 7) on the concave side of the umbrella of a *Tiaropsis indicans* with a needle, the manubrium is brought to the stimulated spot (Fig. 7), as though the animal wished to remove the stimulating object (2). This movement takes place as follows: A bending of the manubrium as well as of the bell ensues in that meridian of the um-

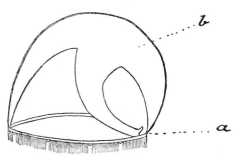

FIG. 7. LOCALISING REFLEX IN TIAROPSIS INDICANS.

If the point *a* on the margin is stimulated, the manubrium is brought to the stimulated spot, somewhat as a decapitated frog tries to wipe off a drop of acetic acid with its foot.

brella which passes through the stimulated point *a*. It seems as though all the muscle-fibres coöperated in bringing the manubrium to the stimulated spot. The central nervous system has nothing to do with this reaction, for Romanes found that it continued after excision of the whole margin with the nerve-ring. On the other hand, if we make an incision in the umbrella parallel to the margin and stimulate a spot below the line of incision, movements of the manubrium, although not pronounced ones, appear in the direction of the quadrant where the stimulated spot is located, but an exact localisation is impossible. Romanes concludes from this that there are radial lines of differentiated tissue passing through all parts of the bell and that it is their function to transmit impressions to the manubrium. He assumes that this tissue is of a nervous character. I believe that the whole phenomenon can be explained without the assumption of a special differentiation of nervous tissue in radial directions. It seems to me that the following assumption is possible: Every localised stimulus leads to an increase in the muscular tension on all sides, which is most intense near the stimulated spot. Now if we decompose each of the lines of increase of tension (aa' ab' ac' ad' ae', Fig. 8) radiating from the stimulated spot, into a meridional component aa' dd' bb', etc., and an equatorial component, it is evident that the latter can have no influence on the manubrium. Only the meridional components can have an influence, and of these the one passing through the stimulated spot is the largest. This fact must necessarily cause a bending of the manubrium toward the stimulated spot. It also shows why an incision parallel to the margin of the umbrella makes an exact localisation impossible and only allows uncertain movements towards the stimulated quadrant.

I hardly believe that the mechanisms for the

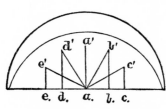

Fig. 8. Diagram for Explaining the Localising Reflex in Medusæ. (See text.)

analogous reflex in a frog or turtle are of a more complicated character. Nature works with very simple tools. The tool employed in the reflex of localisation is the curvature produced by stimulation,— contact, for instance. We meet with this in its simplest form in plants, in which the side that comes in contact with a solid body becomes concave. Plants certainly possess no central nervous system containing mysterious reflex structures. In their case, irritability and conductibility suffice as an explanation. In Medusæ the method appears more complicated only in so far as in them the contractile tissue is real muscle-fibre. In the frog, the only further complication is the fact that the conduction takes place through a special kind of tissue—namely, nerve-tissue. In its first anlage, this central nervous system is of a very simple segmental character. I believe that the central nervous system preserves this simple character better than any other tissue. The muscles undergo considerable displacement during the development, but the changes occurring in the central nervous system by no means equal those occurring in the muscular system.

It seems thus possible to explain the above-mentioned phenomena of coördination in Medusæ by means of the simple facts of irritability and conductivity without attributing any other functions to the ganglion-cell except those which occur in all conducting protoplasm.

3

BIBLIOGRAPHY

1. O. *u.* R. HERTWIG. *Das Nervensystem und die Sinnesorgane der Medusen.*

2. ROMANES, G. J. *Jellyfish, Starfish and Sea Urchins.* The International Science Series, 1893.

3. LOEB, J. *On the Different Effects of Ions upon Myogenic and Neurogenic Rhythmical Contractions,* etc., *American Journal of Physiology,* vol. iii., 1900.

4. LOEB, J. *Ueber Ionen, welche rhythmische Zuckungen der Skelettmuskeln hervorrufen. Festschrift für Fick.* Braunschweig, 1899.

5. QUINCKE. *Ueber periodische Ausbreitung an Flüssigkeitsoberflächen,* etc. *Sitzungsberichte der Berliner Akademie der Wissensch.,* 1888, ii., S. 791.

6. PORTER, W. T. *The Coördination of the Ventricle. The American Journal of Physiology,* vol. ii., 1899.

CHAPTER III

THE CENTRAL NERVOUS SYSTEM OF ASCIDIANS AND ITS SIGNIFICANCE IN THE MECHANISM OF REFLEXES

1. If we wished to observe the order of the natural system in this book, we should not let the Ascidians follow the Medusæ. We consider it more profitable, however, to discuss simple cases before taking up the more complicated ones. Having reached the conclusion, at the end of the preceding chapter, that the spontaneous coördinated activities in Medusæ are not due to specific morphological structures of the ganglion-cells, we will now attempt to find out whether the reflex actions of animals depend upon the structure of the central nervous system or of the peripheral parts. In Ascidians the central nervous system consists of a single ganglion (*d*, Fig. 9). This ganglion is situated between the oral and aboral tubes (*a* and *b*, Fig. 9).

Ciona intestinalis (Fig. 9), a large, transparent Ascidian, possesses a very characteristic reflex. If either the oral or aboral opening be touched, both openings close, and the whole animal contracts so

that it becomes small and round.   This reflex is determined by two groups of muscles, first by ring-
muscles in the oral and aboral openings, second by
longitudinal muscles,
which run lengthwise
through the animal. By
the contraction of these
muscles the animal is
protected from the en-
trance of foreign bodies
into the body cavity.
This reaction is a typ-
ical reflex act, and is
eminently purposeful.
According to the pre-
vailing ideas concern-
ing the decisive rôle
that the ganglion plays
in reflexes, the pro-
cedure is as follows :

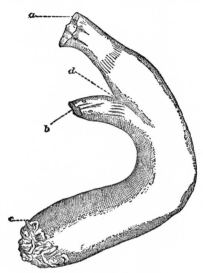

Fig. 9.   Ciona Intestinalis.

a oral, *b* aboral opening ; *c*, foot, *d*, location of
ganglion.

If the oral or aboral
opening be touched, the stimulation is conducted
through the peripheral nerves to the ganglion, where
a mysterious reflex mechanism is brought into play,
which gives the muscles the command to contract in
a manner corresponding to the nature of the stimulus.
Ferrier, for instance, in his text-book, mentions the
one ganglion of the Ascidians as illustrative of the
significance of the ganglion in reflexes.

I removed the ganglion from a number of Cionæ.

For some time after the operation, in most cases for about twenty-four hours, the animals remained contracted. At the end of this period they began to relax again. To my great surprise, I found that the typical reflex continued. If we let a drop of water fall on such an animal, the typical reflex act is produced just as in the normal animal. Hence the reflex cannot be determined by specific structures of the ganglion. But what does determine the reflexes, and what is the function of the ganglion?

The answer to the first question must be that the reflex is determined by the structure and arrangement of the peripheral parts, especially the muscles. The mechanical stimulus throws the muscles directly into activity, and the stimulation is transmitted from muscle-element to muscle-element directly, as in the heart or the ureter. But is the central nervous system superfluous in this animal? We get the answer to this question if we determine the threshold of stimulation. The threshold of stimulation for producing this reflex is higher in animals which have been operated upon than in normal animals. As the source of the stimulus, I used the kinetic energy of drops of water, which fell from a pipette upon the animal. Since the weight of the falling drop in the pipette is always the same, the minimum of the height from which a falling drop can produce a contraction is a convenient measure of the irritability; the latter is of course equal to the reciprocal value of the threshold of stimulation. In one case there were in an aquarium (equally near the surface), a Ciona freshly operated upon and a normal Ciona. The minimum height from which a contraction could be produced was as follows for the normal animal (*a*) and the animal operated upon (*b*) :

a (normal)	*b* (operated)
8 *mm*	65 *mm*
4 *mm*	75 *mm*
10 *mm*	80 *mm*
	80 *mm*

In two other animals used for the experiment I obtained the following values :

a (normal)	*b* (operated)
6 *mm*	22 *mm*
8 *mm*	20 *mm*

It seems to me that the difference in the irritability arises from the fact that in the normal Ascidian the stimulation is conducted through the nerves and the ganglion, in which case less energy is required. In the Ascidian operated upon, however, the muscles are stimulated directly, and the conduction of the stimulation probably takes place from muscle-cell to muscle-cell, just as in the heart. We know, moreover, that the direct irritability of muscle-fibres is not so great as that of the nerves. Hence *the nerves and the ganglion only play the part of a more sensitive and quicker conductor for the stimulus* (1).

2. It may seem as though no conclusions could be drawn from these cases in regard to the " reflex

centres" of higher animals. It is frequently stated that in higher animals the ganglia have assumed functions which in lower animals can be performed by the peripheral organs. It is similarly stated that the higher the animal ranks in the natural system, the more the functions "migrate" toward the cerebral hemispheres. But how such an upward migration of functions is conceivable, none of these authors attempt to explain. It can easily be shown, however, that conditions are the same in higher and lower animals. We must only be careful to homologise a lower form with a single organ or segment of a higher animal. When the intensity of the light is suddenly increased, the pupil of our eye becomes narrower. The sphincter of the iris contracts, and the rays of light are excluded just as foreign bodies are shut out by the contraction of the sphincters in the Ascidians. In the eye, just as in the Ascidian, we have to deal with a typical reflex act. The increased intensity of the light stimulates the retina. The stimulation passes through the optic nerve to its centres, and is carried from there by means of the oculomotorius nerve to the sphincter of the iris, which contracts. It would nevertheless be wrong to assume that the centre for the pupillary reflex plays any other part in this process than that of a protoplasmic connection between the retina and the iris. It has been shown by Arnold, and later by Brown-Séquard and Budge, that even in the excised iris the pupil still contracts when the light strikes the former. I myself have often observed in sharks, whose brain I had removed, that light caused the pupil to contract several hours after death, when signs of decomposition had already begun to appear. Steinach has proved that in this case the muscle-elements in the iris are stimulated directly by the light (3). This reflex is therefore determined by the muscles of the iris, and the nervous connections serve only as quicker and more sensitive conductors. Thus we see that the eyeball behaves toward light just as the Ascidian behaves toward mechanical stimuli.

Some physiologists seem to doubt that the muscles can be stimulated directly by light without the intervention of the ganglion-cells. But we know that phenomena of contraction are also produced by the light in the unicellular swarmspores of algæ, which certainly contain no ganglia. Furthermore, no one doubts that muscles without ganglion-cells can also be stimulated chemically or mechanically. Why should there not also be muscle-fibres that can be stimulated directly by light? There is no reason for assuming that all muscles must behave exactly like the muscles of the frog's leg, simply because the experiments on it have by chance furnished the prevailing views concerning muscles.

The reader may believe that the pupillary reflex is an exceptional case, but this is not true. Defæcation and urination in higher animals may be considered as reflex phenomena of the spinal cord. The pressure of the fæces or of the urine acts as a stimulus, which affects the centres for the activity of the muscles of these organs, and this stimulation is said to cause the contracted sphincters to relax. Goltz and Ewald have found, however, that after extirpation of the entire spinal cord up to the cervical part, defæcation and urination still occur normally (4). Only for a time after the operation the sphincters are relaxed. Later on everything again becomes normal. These phenomena probably belong to the same class as the one already described in the Ascidian. The processes in the normal evacuations of the bladder and rectum are not determined by the morphological structure of the so-called reflex centre, but by the muscles of the bladder and of the rectum themselves. The spinal cord serves only as a more sensitive and quicker conductor for the stimulus. Goltz and Ewald are inclined, it is true, to assume that, after all, ganglion-cells or unknown nervous structures determine these results. But the fact that the muscles of the skeleton can be caused to contract rhythmically when put in the right solution, makes this assumption unnecessary; moreover, the facts of comparative physiology must also be taken into consideration. The *Actinia mesembryanthemum* of the East Sea and the Mediterranean perhaps show fewer differences morphologically than the sphincter ani and the gastrocnemius, and yet the *Actinia mesembryanthemum* of the Mediterranean shows a form of irritability which the Actinian of the same name from the East Sea does not show, namely, negative geotropism. I mention this illustration, to which many others might be added, in order to show that forms which are morphologically alike need not necessarily be alike in all their reactions. Experiments on fermentation show that a small stereochemical difference of a carbohydrate or proteid can produce an entirely different physiological effect.

The possibility, of course, remains that scattered ganglion-cells exist in Ascidians under the epidermis just as in Medusæ. Mr. Hunter, who has studied the nervous system of Ascidians, informs us that he has found cells in certain places under the epidermis of Ascidians which he believes to be ganglion-cells. But after all that has been said about the scattered ganglion-cells in Hydromedusæ (see page 19) and their rôle in rhythmical contractions, it is not necessary to consider the importance of scattered ganglion-cells for reflexes. Schaper has recently made an observation which makes it seem as though in the young larvæ of Amphibians conditions similar to those in Ascidians exist. He amputated the brain of the larva of a frog during the first days of development, and saw that the animal was still able to move spontaneously seven days after the operation. When sections of the animal were made, it was found that the spinal cord had also perished (2). This observation should be repeated and enlarged upon. It is quite possible that during the first days of development a direct transmission of the waves of stimulation may take place from the skin to the muscles in the larva of the frog, without the intervention of the central nervous system, as happens in the Ascidians.

3. The objection might now be raised that the bladder and rectum are minor organs of the body. But what has been said above concerning them also holds good for larger and more important groups of organs, namely for the blood-vessels. These are able to adapt their width to external conditions; the vessels of the skin become dilated when a loss of heat is desirable, and they contract in the cold when the loss of heat should be reduced. It is assumed that the mechanisms for these purposeful reflexes are contained in the central nervous system. Goltz and Ewald (4) have found, however, that dogs which have lost the spinal cord almost up to the medulla oblongata live for years. This alone proves that the blood-vessels can adapt themselves to the external temperature, independently of the central nervous system. Goltz had already proved that the blood-vessels regain their tonus if all the nerves of a limb be severed, the limb being connected with the animal only by means of the blood-vessels. The same thing occurs after extirpation of the spinal cord. The temperature of the hind-paws of animals whose spinal cord has been destroyed up to the thoracic part becomes normal again after the operation—that is to say, the hind-paws have the same temperature as the fore-paws which remain connected with the central nervous system. If we hold the hand in snow for a time, we observe as a local after-effect a relaxation of the muscles of the blood-vessels and an increase in the temperature of the hand. Goltz and

Ewald were able to show that the same phenomena may also be observed when the hind-legs of dogs whose spinal cord has been destroyed are packed for a time in snow.

From the standpoint of human physiology these results seem strange, but from that of comparative physiology they are readily understood. The various reactions of plants to external stimuli are just as purposeful as those of animals. Why should it not be possible, then, for single organs and tissues of higher animals to react purposefully to external stimuli, and is there any reason why the purposeful character of a reaction should be dependent upon the structure of the central nervous system?

We have been able to rid ourselves of erroneous views concerning the significance of the ganglia of the central nervous system in higher animals through the help of the Ascidians; they also help us further to determine the true rôle of the nervous system. Although the dogs experimented upon by Goltz and Ewald were able to adapt the width of their blood-vessels to the variations of temperature, it was necessary to shield them much more carefully from sudden changes of temperature than is necessary in the case of normal animals. The threshold of stimulation was raised and probably the rapidity of the conduction decreased. For this reason, dogs whose spinal cord is destroyed are no longer fit to live out-of-doors. As regards regulation of temperature, they are like an intoxicated person, and would perish in the cold much sooner than a normal animal. Hence the nervous system does not contain any regulating mechanisms, but it serves as a quicker conductor, and allows the peripheral organs to work with greater precision.

4. Bethe has recently made a difficult experiment on *Carcinus mænas*, which, however, was successful in only two cases. If this experiment is correct, it proves that, in the conduction of a reflex in the central nervous system, the process of conduction does not of necessity pass through the ganglion-cell itself (5). An anatomical observation caused Bethe to perform this operation. " Almost all the ganglion-cells of Carcinus are unipolar, and often the axis-cylinder of the cell runs for a long distance before it gives off the first dendrites and sends out the peripheral fibre. It seemed very strange to me that a stimulus entering through the sensory nerves into the central organ should go through the dendrites to the far-distant motor-ganglion cells, and travel the great part of the same path before entering the peripheral motor fibre, instead of going directly to the motor fibre. It was easy to decide this question by separating the ganglion-cells with their axis-cylinder process from the motor neurons without injuring the neuropiles. If the ganglion-cell were absolutely essential for the reflex, the muscles involved should become paralysed immediately after the operation ; if it were not essential, no paralysis should occur, at least for some time, and the stimulus could go across

directly from the dendrites to the peripheral fibre." It was possible to perform the operation in Carcinus on the ganglion-cells which innervate the muscles of the second antenna. The cutting of the peripheral nerves (*Antennarius secundus*) that go to these ganglion-cells immediately causes a complete paralysis of the antennæ, a proof that the fibres of these nerves are the only conductors of the stimulus which can call forth a reflex movement of these antennæ. But when Bethe removed the ganglion-cells, without injuring the neuropile of the second antenna, "the second antenna retained its tonus and its reflex irritability. It does not hang down limp, but remains stiff and in the normal position. When stimulated, it is withdrawn, but is stretched out again when the stimulation ceases. From this it is evident that the ganglion-cells are not necessary for reflexes. The reflex arc either does not pass through the ganglion-cells or does not need to pass through them. It is further apparent that the ganglion-cell has nothing to do with the tonus of the muscles, and that the permanent influence which the central nervous system exercises upon the tension of the muscles is not produced in the ganglion-cells (6)."

This experiment, even if it be correct, adds nothing of importance to our conclusions. If the reflex arc acts only as a quick protoplasmic conductor, the question whether the stimulus has to pass through the ganglion itself or not becomes of secondary importance.

BIBLIOGRAPHY.

1. LOEB, J. *Untersuchungen zur physiologischen Morphologie der Thiere.* II. Würzburg, 1892, S. 37.

2. SCHAPER, A. *Experimentelle Studien an Amphibienlarven. Archiv für Entwicklungsmechanik,* Bd. vi., 1898.

3. STEINACH, E. *Untersuchungen zur vergleichenden Physiologie der'Iris. Pflüger's Archiv,* Bd. lii., 1892.

4. GOLTZ und EWALD. *Der Hund mit verkürztem Rückenmark. Pflüger's Arch.,* Bd. lxiii., 1896.

5. BETHE, A. *Das Centralnervensystem von Carcinus mænas.* I. Theil, II. Mittheilung. *Archiv f. mikroskop. Anatomie und Entwicklungsgeschichte,* Bd. 1., 1897.

6. BETHE, A. *Das Centralnervensystem von Carcinus mænas.* II. Theil. *Arch. f. mikroskop. Anatomie und Entwicklungsgeschichte,* Bd. li., 1898.

CHAPTER IV

EXPERIMENTS ON ACTINIANS

1. The two preceding chapters have furnished proof of the fact that the phenomena of purposeful reflex action, of spontaneity, and of coördination are determined, not by *specific* characters of the ganglion-cells, but by general peculiarities common to all protoplasm. These peculiarities are irritability and the power of conducting stimuli, both of which will find their explanation in the physics of colloidal substances.

In this chapter we wish to put the foregoing conclusions to a test by showing that a group of animals without any true central nervous system are able to show reactions complex as those in higher animals. Without such a parallel we should be more than ready, in the case of higher animals, to attribute such reactions to the specific structure of the ganglia or the ganglion-cells.

We cannot speak of a central nervous system in Actinians in the same sense as in Ascidians. Under the ectoderm there are elements which are interpreted by some authors as ganglion-cells and nerve-fibres.

The unreliability of this interpretation is apparent, however, from the fact that Claus considers it uncertain. He mentions the possibility of a conduction of stimuli as one of the conditions that speak for the existence of a nervous system in Actinians. But a con-

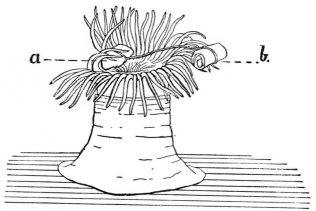

FIG. 10. THE ABILITY OF THE ACTINIANS TO DISCRIMINATE.
The tentacles press the meat *a* into the mouth, while they drop the water-soaked paper *b*.

duction of stimuli also occurs in plants. During the year 1888 in Kiel, and 1889–90 in Naples, I made investigations on the reactions of Actinians, which show how little reason we have for concluding that complicated reactions need depend upon similarly complicated reflex centres (1). It is very obvious from these experiments that the structure and irritability of the *peripheral organs* determine the reactions. We will begin with the description of experiments on the *Actinia equina* (*mesembryanthemum*) of the East Sea.

4

If a wad of paper soaked in sea-water be placed on the mouth of one of these Actinians it is refused, while a piece of crab-meat, which to us does not differ in taste from the wad of paper, is usually accepted without delay. I tied one end of a short thread around a

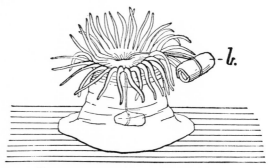

FIG. 11. CONTINUATION OF THE EXPERIMENT IN FIG. 10.

paper wad and the other end around a piece of meat, and threw both on the outstretched tentacles of a starved Actinian. The tentacles that came in contact with the meat (*a*, Fig. 10) reacted at once by bending in such a way as to bring the meat to the mouth, while the tentacles that were in contact with the paper did not react. I withdrew the thread and placed it on the oral disc in such a way that the paper rested on the tentacles where the meat had rested before, and *vice versa*. The meat was then drawn into the mouth and the string with it, but the paper remained outside the oral opening (Fig. 11). During the next twenty-four hours no change took place ; later on, the thread was ejected without the meat. The latter was probably digested. I have often repeated the experiment, always obtaining the same result, except that occasionally the string was ejected sooner, in which case the meat remained on the string, partially or entirely undigested. These phenomena have the same explanation as the behaviour of insect-eating plants. The chemical substances diffusing from the meat, together with the tactile stimuli exerted by it, cause a bending of the tentacles that are touched in such a way that they become concave and carry the meat toward the oral opening. The contact of the meat with the mouth causes the sphincter of the oral opening to relax; the pressure of the tentacles, together with the activity of the oral disc, then pushes the meat into the interior of the digestive tract. But if these specific chemical stimuli are wanting, if we give the animal, for instance, water-soaked filter-paper, the contractions of those muscles which carry the tentacles to the mouth are not produced. The tentacles remain relaxed or relax still more under the stimulus, and this fact, together with the ciliary movement, causes the paper wad to fall off.

2. It is said that the nerve-elements are much more numerous in the vicinity of the mouth than in any other part of the animal. One might think that this concentration of nerve-elements determined the reflex mechanism for these reactions. For this reason, I have made use of results obtained while carrying on investigations concerning heteromorphosis. I had found that in an Actinian of the Mediterranean,

Cerianthus membranaceus, new tentacles could be produced by a lateral incision in the body of the animal. But in some of these cases no *mouth* is formed. Fig.

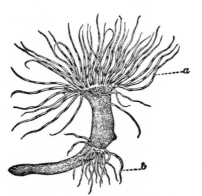

FIG. 12. ACTINIAN (CERIANTHUS) WITH A NORMAL HEAD (*a*) AND AN ARTIFICIALLY PRODUCED HEAD (*b*).

Although the latter has no oral opening the tentacles carry the meat to the place where the mouth ought to be.

12 shows such an animal ; *a* is the normal, *b* the new head. If the incision was very small, only single tentacles were formed, without the oral disc. These new tentacles behave toward food exactly like the tentacles of the old mouth. If we offer such a new head a piece of meat, the tentacles seize and press it against the centre of the oral disc, where the mouth should be. After pressing in vain for some minutes the tentacles relax and the meat falls off. This experiment could be repeated for months, in fact as long as I observed the animal (2). In other cases the second head was so near the old one that it was easy to stimulate the tentacles of both simultaneously with the same piece of meat. In this case a fight arose between the two tentacle systems, each attempting to draw the meat toward its own oral disc. Parker has lately shown that even a single tentacle, after being severed from the animal, grasps a piece of meat and

bends with it toward the place where, in relation to itself, the mouth ought to be (3).

If we look at these facts without prejudice, we must conclude that the reaction of the tentacles is determined only by the irritability of the tentacle-elements themselves, and by the arrangement of their contractile elements. The following observations may also be considered in support of this conclusion.

3. If an *Actinia equina* be divided transversely, the oral piece, which we will call the head-piece, has the normal head, with mouth and tentacles on its oral end ; on its aboral end the body-cavity is open to the exterior, and food may pass through the opening in either direction. The old mouth of a head-piece was as particular as usual in regard to the selection of its food, while the aboral end readily swallowed pieces of paper. The old mouth often refused meat, but the aboral mouth was almost always ready to accept it, even when it would refuse paper.

I laid a piece of an Actinian that took food in at both ends on its side, and tried to find out whether both mouths would take food simultaneously. I first placed a piece of meat on the aboral mouth, in order to cause it to open. As soon as this happened and the meat was being taken into the mouth I offered the oral mouth also a piece, and this was likewise accepted. The act of swallowing in the other mouth was interrupted at once by the contraction of the ring-muscles. After a few moments, however, when the meat in the oral mouth had been swallowed, the muscles of the aboral end relaxed and the meat taken in before by this mouth fell out. When I fed the mouths *in succession*, the mouth that was fed first ejected the food as soon as the other began to eat. It is obvious from this that a peristaltic wave is started from the end which takes up food.

Thus far we have considered only the head-piece. If we turn our attention now to the foot-piece, we find that on the oral end a new oral disc with tentacles soon begins to form. Before this has occurred, however, the mouth takes pieces of meat and swallows them. It seemed to me as though this new mouth, even before the regeneration of the oral disc, resembled the normal mouth more than the aboral mouth in the head-piece, for it did not accept paper wads and grains of sand, while it swallowed meat well.

4. In the foot of the Actinians the contact-irritability is of special interest. The foot of a normal *Actinia equina* attaches itself to the surface of solid bodies. The character of the surface is of great importance for producing these processes of attachment. If it finds no other body, the Actinian attaches itself to the glass of the aquarium, and glides about on it. If, however, the shell of a Mytilus is placed in the aquarium and the animal comes in contact with it while moving about, it immediately attaches itself to the shell, and remains there, whether the shell is empty or inhabited. The surface of an ulva leaf has the same effect. While the animal upon contact with

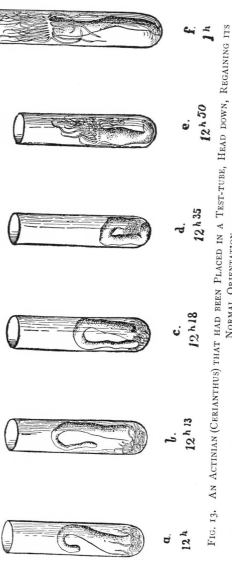

a.
12ʰ

b.
12ʰ13

c.
12ʰ18

d.
12ʰ35

e.
12ʰ50

f.
1ʰ

FIG. 13. AN ACTINIAN (CERIANTHUS) THAT HAD BEEN PLACED IN A TEST-TUBE, HEAD DOWN, REGAINING ITS NORMAL ORIENTATION.

The animal was placed in the tube shortly before twelve o'clock. At twelve the tip of the foot began to bend downward (a). Eighteen minutes later the foot had reached the bottom of the tube (c). At twelve thirty-five the head began to be raised (d), and at one o'clock the Actinian had regained its normal orientation (f).

55

the ulva leaf will at any time leave the glass and attach itself to the leaf, the reverse is not liable to happen. *This contact-irritability of the foot does not change if the head or the greater oral part of the animal be amputated.* The mechanisms for the discharge of these reactions must, therefore, be located in the foot itself and not in the ganglion-cells of the oral disc.

5. In higher animals we recognise a tendency to give the body a certain orientation in space. We usually call such an orientation in a higher animal its position of equilibrium. Certain Actinians also show such phenomena. If we put a Cerianthus into a test-tube filled with sea-water, and place the glass so that the head of the animal is down, the foot up, and the longitudinal axis vertical, the tip of the foot will begin after a few moments to bend downward vertically. In Fig. 13 the course of such an experiment is given from life. Some minutes before 12 o'clock the animal was placed in the test-tube in the manner described above. At 12 o'clock the foot had begun to bend downward (Fig. 13, *a*); in the next thirteen minutes the bending toward the head had progressed (*b*); five minutes later the foot had reached the bottom of the tube (*c*). The bending progressed steadily to new elements lying near the head; and since the foot now stood upon the bottom of the tube, the farther advance of the curvature toward the head resulted in the lifting of the latter (Fig. 13, *d* and *e*), whereupon the animal raised itself bodily, and at 1 o'clock had the position *f*. The process of righting

required one hour. The animal remained in this position for two days, and then crawled out of the glass.

In analysing the conditions that determine the righting of the Cerianthus in this case, two circum-

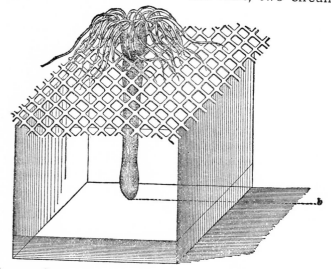

FIG. 14. CERIANTHUS REGAINING ITS NORMAL ORIENTATION.

It was placed on the net horizontally, and within half an hour had regained its normal vertical position, by pushing itself through the meshes of the net.

stances must be taken into consideration, namely, gravitation and the contact-stimuli. It can be easily shown that gravitation alone is able to produce the above-mentioned reaction of the Cerianthus. A wire net, whose meshes are so fine that the body of a Cerianthus can only be drawn through them by force, is laid horizontally upon a glass standing in the aquarium. A Cerianthus is laid on the wire net. After a few minutes the foot of the animal begins to bend downward and to work its way through one of the meshes of the net. In the oral pole no change takes place except that the tentacles lay themselves close together, so that they look like a brush whose handle is formed by the body of the animal. The animal forces its body farther and farther through the meshes until it is at last able to keep itself in a vertical position as represented in Fig. 14. This orientation can be reached in half an hour. If we turn the wire net over as soon as the animal has reached the position represented in Fig. 14, so that the foot is up, it does not pull itself out of the net again, but the foot near the tip begins to bend downward vertically. The bending then progresses from element to element of the body, from the foot toward the head, until the tip of the foot reaches the wire net, when it again pushes itself through as far as possible. If the wire net be turned over again, the process is repeated. Thus the animal can be forced, simply with the aid of gravitation, to weave itself in and out of the net. Fig. 15 shows a Cerianthus that has been forced to push itself through three times in this manner. The drawing was made from life. In these experiments we have an example of a geotropic irritability,—in other words, of positive geotropism. As this kind of irritability is very common in the roots of plants, it follows that for the mechanism of these reactions no specific qualities of the ganglion-cells are necessary. If a transverse incision be made in the middle of a Cerianthus which almost but not quite separates the two halves, and the animal be placed immediately after the operation on a wire net, the foot works itself into one of the meshes up as far as the incision and assumes a vertical position. The oral piece, on the contrary, from the place of incision to the head, usually remains lying horizontally on the net. This shows that the foot possesses geotropic irritability.

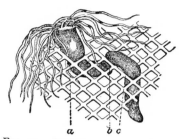

FIG. 15. ACTINIAN THAT HAS BEEN FORCED BY GRAVITATION TO PUSH ITSELF THROUGH THE NET THREE TIMES (*a*, *b*, AND *c*). See text.

But if the Actinian be divided transversely we see that the head-piece as well as the tail-piece pushes itself through the meshes, although not so frequently.

While an Actinian that is suspended vertically in a test-tube or in a mesh of a wire net seldom retains this position longer than two days, it remains indefinitely in the sand after burrowing. In addition to gravitation, some other stimulus must hold it there. I believe that it is the contact-stimulus of the sand. I called this kind of irritability stereotropism, and have shown that in a series of animals it determines their habits. Positive geotropism and positive stereotropism cause the Cerianthi to burrow in the sand vertically, and the positive stereotropism keeps them permanently in the burrow.

We see from this that quite complicated reactions occur in these animals although they do not possess a central nervous system like that in higher animals. Were we to come across these same reactions in higher animals we should be inclined *a priori* to ascribe them to the complicated structure of the central nervous system. The experiments on Actinians will perhaps prevent us from drawing such a conclusion before we have forcible reasons for so doing. A high degree of complication in the reactions of animals can be reached where no central nervous system exists, or where it serves only as a sensitive and quick protoplasmic conductor. The *cause* of complicated reactions lies, therefore, in the irritabilities and structures of the peripheral organs.

BIBLIOGRAPHY.

1. LOEB, J. *Untersuchungen zur physiologischen Morphologie der Thiere*, I., 1891. Würzburg, G. Hertz.

2. LOEB, J. *Zur Physiologie und Psychologie der Aktinien. Pflüger's Archiv*, Bd. lix., 1895.

3. PARKER, G. H. *The Reactions of Metridium to Food and Other Substances. Bulletin of the Museum of Comparative Zoölogy at Harvard College*, vol. xxix., 1896.

4. POLLOCK, W. H. *On Indications of the Sense of Smell in Actiniæ. Jour. Linnean Soc.*, London, vol. xvi., 1882.

5. NAGEL, W. *Experimentelle sinnesphysiologische Untersuchungen an Coelenteraten. Pflüger's Archiv*, Bd. lvii., 1894.

CHAPTER V

EXPERIMENTS ON ECHINODERMS

1. The nervous system of the starfish consists, first, of a central nerve-ring around the mouth (Fig. 16), and, second, of the peripheral nerves radiating from this ring into each of the arms.

It is a well-known fact that if such an animal be laid on its back it soon rights itself. In species like that represented in Fig. 16 the ambulacral feet found on the ventral surface in great numbers execute the righting. These little feet are muscular tubes, which end in a plate. By means of this plate the foot, like the sucker of the leech, can cling to solid bodies. If a starfish be laid on its back, the tube-feet of all the arms

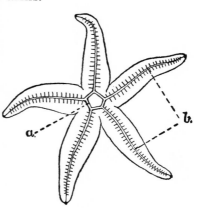

FIG. 16. NERVOUS SYSTEM OF A STARFISH.

a, central nerve-ring that surrounds the mouth, *b*, peripheral nerves of the arms.

are stretched out at once and are moved hither and thither as if feeling for something, and soon the tips of one or more arms turn over and touch the underlying surface with their ventral side (Fig. 17). The tube-feet of these arms attach themselves to this

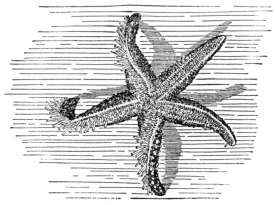

FIG. 17. MECHANISM OF THE TURNING OF A STARFISH THAT HAS
BEEN LAID ON ITS BACK.

The tube-feet of the three arms at the left are pulling while the other two arms are quiet.
This causes the animal to turn a somersault toward the left which brings it again into
the natural position.

surface, and the animal is then able to turn a somersault and regain its normal position. For this result, it is essential that all five arms do not attempt simultaneously to bring the animal into the ventral position. Should the tips of all five, or even four, arms tug simultaneously, it would be impossible for the animal to turn over. In normal starfish having five arms, not more than three begin the act of turning; the other two remain quiet. If we, however, destroy the nervous connection between the arms, for instance, by making two incisions at *a* and *b*, Fig. 18, this coöperation of the arms ceases. The normal starfish requires but a few minutes to turn over, but the specimen represented in Fig. 18 remained on its

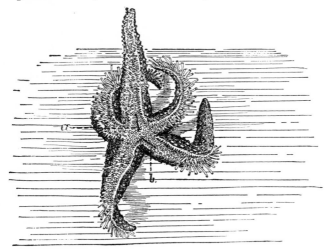

FIG. 18. THE SAME EXPERIMENT ON A STARFISH WHOSE NERVE-RING HAS BEEN SEVERED IN TWO PLACES (*a* AND *b*).

The right and left arms are consequently no longer connected nervously. If such an animal is laid on its back, the tube-feet of four or even all the arms in most cases tug simultaneously. This prevents the animal from righting itself.

back the whole afternoon, although the arms were struggling constantly to right it. The experiments seem to indicate that in a normal starfish the stimulus produced by the pulling of two or three arms in the same direction has an inhibitory effect on the other arms. This inhibition ceases when the nervous connection between the single arms is broken. Romanes found that a single arm containing only the peripheral arm-nerve rights itself when laid on its back. Hence the central nerve-ring acts only as a conductor and not as a " centre " for this reaction (1).

2. In analysing this righting reflex of the starfish, there are two possibilities to be considered. Either gravity forces the starfish to turn the ventral side toward the centre of the earth, or contact-irritability, *i. e.*, stereotropism, forces the animal to bring the ventral side in contact with solid bodies. The fact that the animals leave the horizontal bottom of an aquarium and attach themselves to the vertical sides shows that gravity is not the cause. Preyer made an experiment from which he concluded that the righting of the starfish is due to their being forced to have the ventral side down. He suspended a starfish in the middle of the aquarium by fastening each of its arms by threads to a cork that floated on the surface of the aquarium. If suspended with its back down, Preyer noticed that the starfish turned over. This might suggest the idea that the righting of the starfish is a geotropic phenomenon. I have repeated Preyer's experiment and confirmed his observation (2). At the same time, however, I made a control experiment which Preyer omitted. In the beginning I fastened the starfish to the cork-plate in such a way that the ventral side was turned toward the bottom. But the starfish even then turned over. This shows that the suspension makes it restless and causes it to perform all sorts of turning movements. I believe

that the ventral side of the starfish is positively stereotropic, or, in other words, that the starfish becomes
restless if its ambulacral feet are not in contact with
solid bodies.

3. Preyer accredits the starfish with possessing
" intelligence." He placed one arm of an Ophiuris
in a piece of rubber tubing in order to see whether
the animal would be clever enough to rid itself of this
impediment to its movements. He found that after
a time the arm " freed itself " from the tube. I have
repeated the experiment in these animals and found
that the Ophiuris pays no attention to the rubber
tube. The animal of course loses it after a time unless it fits too closely, but it is always purely a matter
of chance, and there is no more intelligence involved
than the clothes-line displays when the clothes are
blown from it by the wind. Romanes found that
when one arm of a starfish is stimulated the animal
moves in a direction opposite to the stimulated arm.
This also looks like intelligence, for the animal seems
to be able to avoid a danger. The late Professor
Norman called my attention to the fact that when
one arm of a starfish is stimulated the feet of this
arm are drawn in and the arm becomes inactive.
This is, however, only true of the stimulated arm ;
the others remain active. Therefore, according to the
parallelogram of forces, a movement away from the
point of stimulation will take place. Intelligence
plays no part in this phenomenon.

4. The tendency to crawl upwards on vertical

5

surfaces is a pronounced reaction of Echinoderms and is quite common in other animals, for instance in the *Actinia mesembryanthemum* of the Mediterranean, and in the Coccinelli. This tendency is also present in plant-organisms — for example, Plasmodia,— and here Sachs has traced it back to negative geotropism. I will repeat here the description which I have already given in a former publication of the phenomenon as it appears among Echinoderms (3).

No one who observes the animals on rocks or posts near the surface of the ocean when the water is quiet can fail to notice the relatively large number of Echinoderms. Many of these—for example, the *Cucumaria cucumis*, which is very common in the Bay of Naples—always live near the surface, not beyond a depth of about 30 m. It can be shown that Cucumaria, like Plasmodia or Coccinelli, are forced, when on vertical surfaces, to crawl upward. Cucumaria has a slender pentagonal body, 10 cm. or more in length, with radial, branching tentacles on its oral end. There are five ridges on the body, and in these are situated longitudinal rows of tube-feet, by means of which the animal crawls upward, even on smooth glass walls. If placed in an aquarium, it crawls about on the bottom until it comes to a vertical side ; it then crawls upward and remains on the highest point, if possible just below the surface of the water. This position then usually becomes permanent, and the animal is converted into a sessile organism.

If a Cucumaria is allowed to attach itself to a

vertical glass which can be revolved around a horizontal axis in the aquarium, it will crawl upward
whenever the glass is turned. This is not a compensatory movement produced by the centrifugal force,
for during the rotation of the glass the animal re-

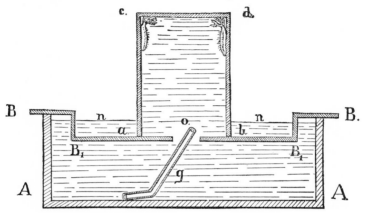

FIG. 19. GEOTROPIC REACTION OF CUCUMARIA CUCUMIS.

The animals are in a battery jar (a, b, c, d). It is filled with water and rests on the bridge
B B in the aquarium A A. Running water is supplied through the tube g at o. They
collect at the highest point (c, d) of the glass.

mains quiet, and not until a quarter or half an hour
after the rotation does it begin to migrate upward.
Neither is the upward migration caused by the light
falling in from above. If the animals are placed in
an aquarium in which light is allowed to enter only
from the side or from below, they will still crawl upward on the vertical sides. In a dark room they behave just as they do in the light.

One might believe that the need of oxygen determined the upward migration of the Cucumariæ to the

surface of the water. It can be shown, however, that this is not the case. If a large beaker filled with water be placed inverted in the aquarium, the Cucumariæ that are under the beaker begin to creep up to the bottom of the glass. They also do so when the experiment is made in the manner represented in Fig. 19. A bridge B B is placed in the aquarium A A, the horizontal part of the bridge B B being below the surface of the water of the aquarium. The horizontal part has a round opening o over which the inverted beaker $a\,b\,c\,d$ filled with water is placed. Fresh water is supplied at a low pressure at o through a glass tube g, which has been properly bent. The Cucumariæ nevertheless go away from o and remain at the highest point $c\,d$, or near $c\,d$ on the vertical sides (Fig. 19), where they ultimately die.

Experiments on the centrifugal machine yielded no result, for the animals did not move during the rotation. Gravity is the only condition which can account for the phenomenon, and I imagine the influence which gravity exercises to be in a manner similar to that observed among insects—for example, in butterflies which have just emerged from the chrysalis. The wings of the butterfly do not unfold immediately, and it runs about restlessly until it comes to a vertical surface. When this is reached, the butterfly creeps upon it and remains there for some time with its head up. After the wings are spread, other conditions cause the animal to be restless again.

Because of this dependence on gravity, the Cucumariæ are of necessity inhabitants of the surface-regions of the ocean. If a larva were carried down to a great depth, its negative geotropism would force it to migrate upward until the highest point was reached or until death put an end to its upward journey.

Certain starfish — for instance *Asterina gibbosa*, which also lives near the surface of the water—behave like Cucumaria. All the experiments I have made on Cucumaria can likewise be successfully performed on *Asterina gibbosa*, but with the difference that the exceptionally voracious Asterina does not remain permanently at the highest point of the vertical surface. In two days, or sometimes even sooner, it begins to move or drops down.

Positive heliotropism naturally has the same effect as negative geotropism. *Asterina tenuispina*, like *Asterina gibbosa*, lives at the surface of the sea. It is not, however, geotropically irritable ; but it is positively heliotropic. I put a large number of specimens of both species in a heap in an aquarium, into which rays of light from one side only fell nearly horizontally. In a short time the two species had parted, the Tenuispinæ crawling off on the floor toward the source of light. The Gibbosæ, scattered about on the bottom of the aquarium in every direction, crawled up the vertical sides without being influenced at all by the light in their movements. In the ocean, where the vertical rays of daylight are chiefly concerned in the orientation of animals, positive heliotropism must drive *Asterina tenuispina* to the surface of the ocean, just as *Asterina gibbosa* is driven there by negative geotropism.

Preyer mentions briefly in his extensive work on *The Movements of the Starfish* the "tendency of these animals to move upwards." "The strong tendency of starfish and brittlestars to go upward cannot be traced back to lack of air, lack of food, changes in temperature or current, or to a desire for light, for they climb up just the same when these conditions are eliminated. Probably some peculiarity of the bottom, or of just that part of the bottom where the animal is, makes it unsuitable for the suction of the tube-feet. The animals can remain there no longer, so they move upwards. But it is possible that parasites, which I have often found in the ambulacral furrows, may cause this upward migration, for as the stimuli produced by them come from below, they might seem to belong to the bottom."

The first sentence in this generalisation is wrong; the light attracts *Asterina tenuispina* upwards. Second, the character of the bottom does not determine the phenomenon. If *Asterina gibbosa* be placed in a cubical box with glass sides, the animals leave the basal horizontal side and crawl up the vertical sides. If the box then be turned 90° around a horizontal axis, the side which is now basal is deserted by the animals. They crawl up and remain on the side which, while horizontal, they had left. Finally, if Preyer believed that parasites force the animals to crawl upward, it is difficult to see why they should not drive the animals down from the vertical side. As a fact, however, *Asterina gibbosa*, as well as *Cucumaria cucumis*, remains on the highest point of the vertical side. I believe it is much nearer the truth to ascribe the vertical upward movements of certain starfish to an action of the force of gravity.

BIBLIOGRAPHY.

1. ROMANES, G. J. *Jelly-fish, Starfish and Sea Urchins.* New York, 1893.
2. PREYER, W. *Ueber die Bewegung der Seesterne. Mittheilungen aus der zoologischen Station zu Neapel*, Bd. vii, S. 96.
3. LOEB, J. *Ueber Geotropismus bei Thieren. Pflüger's Archiv*, Bd. xlix, 1891.

CHAPTER VI

EXPERIMENTS ON WORMS

1. We shall consider separately in this chapter two kinds of worms : first, those in which the ganglia are all crowded together in the head end — *e. g.*, Planarians ; and second, those with a series of segmental ganglia — *e. g.*, Annelids.

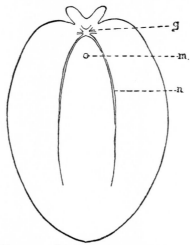

FIG. 20.   THYSANOZOÖN BROCCHII, A MARINE PLANARIAN.

g, brain ; *m*, mouth ; *n*, longitudinal nerve.
(Diagrammatic after Lang.)

Sea- and fresh-water Planarians differ little structurally, yet they may show different reactions upon losing the oral ganglion.

Thysanozoön (Brocchii), Fig. 20, a marine Planarian, is very common in the Bay of Naples. It is from 1 to 3 cm. long and nearly as broad. The oral end of the body, which can be recognised by two tentacles (*g*, Fig. 20), contains the brain of the animal. This consists of two connected ganglia, from which a series of nerves, containing single ganglion-cells, go out ; among the latter, the two large longitudinal nerves running lengthwise throughout the animal (*n*, Fig. 20) are conspicuous. In the periphery a plexus is formed (1). The central nervous system consists of the double ganglion in the forward end. Like all Planarians, Thysanozoön crawls on the side of the aquarium or on the surface film of the water. It differs from the fresh - water Planarians in being able

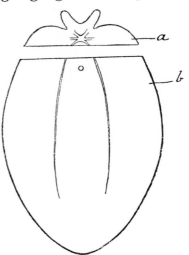

FIG. 21.   THYSANOZOÖN DIVIDED
TRANSVERSELY.

The anterior piece *a*, containing the brain, shows
spontaneity ; the posterior piece *b*, none.

to perform, in addition, genuine swimming movements. With the sides of its body it makes vibrations similar to those made by the wings of a butterfly. If while a Thysanozoön is gliding about on the surface of the water it be divided transversely with a pair of scissors, the posterior or aboral half (*b*, Fig. 21) at once falls to the bottom, while the oral piece (*a*, Fig. 21) containing the brain creeps on undisturbed. If the division be made with a sharp knife while the Planarian is crawling on a glass plate, the oral piece (*a*, Fig. 21) crawls on undisturbed, while the progressive movement of the posterior piece ceases entirely. The spontaneity of the progressive movement of the Thysanozoön is then a function of the part of the body containing the brain (2).

In a Thysanozoön that has been divided, both pieces live and regenerate the lacking parts. The oral piece, however, regenerates more rapidly than the aboral piece, which has to form a head. I have not investigated whether the latter also forms a new brain. I kept such pieces alive for four months. The spontaneity of the posterior piece never returned; the spontaneity of the anterior piece remained.

If we put a normal Thysanozoön on its back it soon rights itself. The question now arises whether, like the progressive movements, these righting movements are a function of the brain. This is not the case. A Thysanozoön from which the brain has been removed rights itself if laid on its back, only the reaction proceeds more slowly than in the normal animal, or even in a piece of an animal if this piece contains the brain. We see here again that the nervous system only serves to bring about a quicker reaction.

If, instead of dividing the Thysanozoön completely, we leave the two parts on one side connected by a thin piece of tissue in such a way that (Fig. 22) the posterior piece can receive no direct innervations from the brain through the longitudinal nerves, conduction of stimuli would still be possible through the side nerve-plexus.

Such an animal was placed after the operation on the bottom of the aquarium ; the anterior piece immediately began to move, while the posterior piece attempted to attach itself to the bottom. The latter soon yielded to the tugging of the oral piece, however, and took part in its progressive movements in an entirely coördinated manner, as though no incision had been made. After a time the oral piece turned around and crawled over the back of the posterior

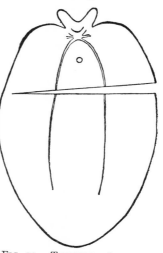

FIG. 22. THYSANOZOÖN WITH TRANSVERSE INCISION.

piece, which was dragged behind passively, and was turned on its back. It righted itself immediately and moved off actively in the same direction as the oral piece. Changes of direction originated only in the piece containing the brain and were never transmitted directly to the posterior piece. But if the oral piece continued for a time to move in the same direction and with the same rapidity, the same movement would soon take place in the posterior piece. Hence the posterior piece did not behave entirely like a piece from which the brain had been removed, for it made progressive movements, nor yet like a normal Thysanozoön for it had lost its spontaneity. This becomes still more apparent from the following observation: I threw a Thysanozoön similarly operated upon into a tank of water. Both pieces performed synchronic swimming movements. The oral piece soon reached the vertical side of the aquarium and began to creep upwards. As a result of the change of direction in the anterior piece, the tissue connecting the two parts became twisted and the back of the posterior piece came in contact with the glass, while the ventral side was turned toward the water. It then made swimming movements and in this way followed the crawling movements of the oral piece. The posterior piece therefore is not simply dragged behind passively, but takes an active part in the progressive movement when the movements are continuous. This is also evident from the fact that it would often crawl along on the back of the oral piece, especially if the latter suddenly began to move more slowly.

These experiments show that a Thysanozoön from which the brain has been removed no longer moves spontaneously, nor is it possible to produce progressive movements in it by any external stimulus. If touched, local contractions, only, result.

2. The brain and nervous system of the fresh-water Planarians (Fig. 23, from Jijima) are so similar to those of the marine Planarians that for our purpose it is unnecessary to give a special description of them. The principal difference is probably that the two longitu-

dinal nerves contain a greater number of ganglion-cells, so that they almost form segmental aggregations. From this similarity we should infer that the brain-functions of the fresh-water Plana-rians would be analogous to those of the Polyclads. However, such is not the case. If we divide a fresh-water Planarian, for instance *Planaria torva*, transversely, the posterior half, that has no brain, crawls just as well as the oral half. Spontaneity in *Planaria torva* is, therefore, by no means a function of the brain. Every piece of the animal that is not too small pos-sesses spontaneity. The decap-itated animals crawl with the anterior end in front like normal animals (2).

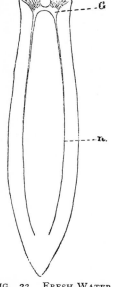

FIG. 23. FRESH-WATER PLANARIAN (PLANA-RIA TORVA).

G, brain, *n*, longitudinal nerve. (After Jijima.)

The question now arises as to how it happens that in Thysano-zoön spontaneous movements cease if the head be amputated, while in fresh-water Planarians this opera-tion does not have such a result. One is tempted to account for the difference by the fact that the fresh-water Planarians have more ganglion-cells throughout the longitudinal nerves than the Thysano-zoön. With the aid of comparative physiology it is possible to show that such a view is untenable. In the crayfish, the suboesophageal ganglion with the ventral ganglion chain represents a much more highly developed ganglion-system than the longitudinal nerves in *Planaria torva*. We shall see, nevertheless, that a crayfish, which possesses these ganglia, but has lost the supraoesophageal ganglion, no longer moves spontaneously. We shall see, furthermore, that a frog that has lost the cerebral hemispheres and thalamus opticus does not move spontaneously, although it possesses many more ganglia in the spinal cord than *Planaria torva*. The same frog, however, moves spontaneously again if, in addition, the optic lobes and the pars commissuralis of the medulla oblongata be removed.

Spontaneous progressive movements are not a specific function of ganglia or of ganglion-cells ; we observe them even in the swarmspores of algæ and in bacteria. Why the decapitated Thysanozoön no longer performs progressive movements, and a decapitated fresh-water Planarian continues to move spontaneously, we are not yet prepared to say. It is possible that the difference between fresh-water and marine Planarians is somewhat of the same character as that between Hydromedusæ and Acalephæ. In the latter, both parts, margin and centre, beat rhythmically in sea-water, while in the Hydromedusæ only the margin with the nerve-ring is able to do so. But we were able to show that this difference between the two classes of Medusæ is not so much due to morphological differences as to chemical or physical differences. A reduction in the amount of Ca ions in the sea-water allowed the centre of a Hydromedusa to beat spontaneously. The case of marine Planarians may be similar, and further experiments may yield the result that with a change in the constitution of the sea-water the posterior half of a Thysanozoön will be able to show spontaneous locomotion.

The behaviour of *Planaria torva* toward light is of special interest. The animal is especially sensitive to changes in the intensity of light. If brought from the dark into the light suddenly, it begins to move. At first the direction of the movements seems to be influenced by the light, for the animals move away from the source of light as if they were negatively heliotropic. However, they do not collect at the point farthest from the source, as do negatively heliotropic animals, but they scatter in all directions and come to rest at last in a place where the light is comparatively weakest. From this it would seem that an increase in the intensity of light causes them to move, while a decrease in the intensity of light causes them to rest. This would account for the fact that we find them by day always under stones or in relatively dark places. I suspect that they begin to move about in the night, and that they come to rest when day returns. I have repeatedly tried the experiment of covering in the morning one-half of the dish with black paper. During the day no change takes place, but the next morning all the animals are found under the covered portion of the dish. The only possible explanation for this behaviour is that they crawl about in the dish during the night and in the morning stop in the darkest place. These animals have at their oral pole not only a brain but also comparatively well-developed eyes. I resolved to try whether a decapitated Planarian, in spite of the loss of brain and eyes, would still show the same reactions toward light as the normal animals. This is the case to a most surprising extent. In the evening, about sixty specimens of *Planaria torva* were cut transversely just behind the brain and eyes. All the pieces were put into a dish with vertical sides which was half covered with black paper. The next morning nearly all the pieces, posterior as well as anterior, were found in the covered portion of the aquarium, where they were scattered about pretty uniformly. In the uncovered portion of the dish I found a few pieces, anterior, however, as well as posterior ones, crowded together in a corner where the intensity of the light was a comparative minimum. Upon repeating this experiment with normal Planarians, the same result was obtained. When the decapitated animals were at rest in the covered portion of the dish, their rest was soon disturbed if, without jarring the aquarium, the dark paper was removed suddenly. At first they crawled about on the side away from the light, then they collected again where the intensity of light was a relative minimum. This reaction occurred just as in normal animals, except that the reaction-time of the brainless animals was greater than in normal animals. In the

pieces containing brain and eyes, the reaction began about one minute after exposure to light ; in the
pieces without brain, after about five minutes.   In this
experiment, only diffused daylight was employed as a
stimulus.   In a round dish with vertical sides, the
Planarians do not collect, like strictly heliotropic animals, on the window- or room-side of the dish, but on
the right and left sides.   Decapitated Planarians behave in the same way.   All these reactions occur the
day after the operation.   Fresh
material should always be used for
these experiments.

After what has been said, it is
hardly necessary to mention that
pieces of *Planaria torva* from which
the brain has been removed right
themselves as well as normal animals.

According to some authors, the
starfish represents a colony of as
many individuals as it has arms.
We have seen that these react har-
moniously as long as the nervous
connection is uninterrupted.   In
Actinians that have been made two-
headed artificially, this harmony no
longer exists ; for instance, in taking food both heads
struggle for the same piece of meat.   At my suggestion, Dr. van Duyne tried to produce multi-headed
Planarians artificially.   He succeeded in making
them with as many as six heads.   Fig. 24 shows a

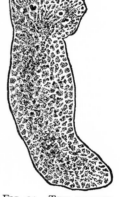

FIG. 24. TWO-HEADED
PLANARIAN PRODUCED
ARTIFICIALLY. (After
van Duyne.)

6

two-headed specimen. If the heads were far enough apart, they no longer moved synchronically in the

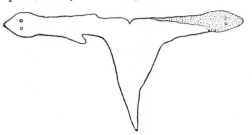

same direction, in which case the pulling in opposite directions (Fig. 25) was so strong that the animal was torn asunder (6).

FIG. 25. PLANARIAN WITH TWO HEADS THAT ARE ATTEMPTING TO MOVE IN OPPOSITE DIRECTIONS, AND IN SO DOING ARE TEARING THE COMMON BODY. (After van Duyne.)

3. In the Annelids we find a segmental arrangement of the central nervous system. This type of structure is also found in Arthropods and in Vertebrates. It will perhaps make our task easier if we conceive the segmented animal to be a colony of as many individuals or animals as there are segments (or ganglia) present in the body. Each segment is then comparable to an Ascidian in which the central nervous system consists of but one ganglion. The fibres and cells of each ganglion form for the corresponding segment a protoplasmic bridge between the skin and muscles. A stimulation beginning, however, in one segment is not confined to that segment, for the single ganglia of the various segments are connected with each other by means of nerve-fibres, the so called longitudinal commissures. By means of these, a stimulation which originates in one segment is transmitted also to the neighbouring

ganglia and from these to those farther away, until at last it reaches the end of the animal.

The central nervous system of Annelids corresponds to the spinal cord of Vertebrates and consists simply of a chain of ganglia. These lie entirely on the ventral side of the animal, with the exception of the most anterior (supracœsophageal) ganglion (Fig. 26), which lies above the œsophagus on the dorsal side. This is connected with the subœsophageal ganglion by a double commissure, which forms a loop through which the œsophagus passes. It may be called the brain, although the small analogy existing between Vertebrates and worms makes the use of the term purely arbitrary.

A question of fundamental interest to us arises at this point : Is the brain simply a segmental ganglion, or is it an organ of a higher order which

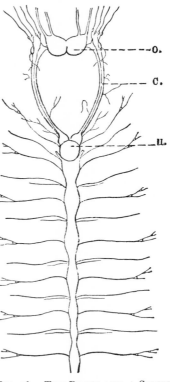

FIG. 26. THE BRAIN AND A SERIES OF SEGMENTAL GANGLIA OF AN ANNELID (NEREIS).

o, supracœsophageal ganglion or brain ; *c*, commissure ; *u*, subœsophageal ganglion. (After Claparède.)

regulates and guides the activity of the other ganglia?

In our analysis of the nerve-functions we will begin with the earthworm. We will consider first its progressive movements, and will attempt to answer the question, Does coördinated progressive movement, in which all the segments of the body participate, depend upon the brain (*o*, Figs. 27 and 28)? The locomotion of the earthworm is a very simple process. The setæ play an important rôle, although they are not visible to the naked eye; they act like locomotor appendages and give the animal a hold on the ground. The real muscles of locomotion, however, are contained in the cutaneous muscle-layer. This consists of ring-fibres

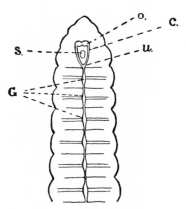

FIG. 27. DORSAL VIEW OF THE CENTRAL NERVOUS SYSTEM OF AN EARTHWORM.

o, supracœsophageal ganglion; *c*, commissure; *u*, subcœsophageal ganglion; *S*, pharynx; *G*, ganglia of the ventral cord.

and longitudinal fibres. When the worm begins to move, the ring-fibres contract first, causing the worm to become longer and thinner. The bristles are turned backward and, because of the resistance of the ground, prevent the animal from moving backward. In this way the head is pushed forward. As soon as the maximum elongation has been reached, the longitudinal muscles contract and the worm becomes shorter. As the bristles are still turned backward, the shortening can only be accomplished by the approach of the posterior end toward the head. The entire worm is therefore compelled to move forward. What happens if we divide the ganglion-chain of the animal in the middle of the body, or if we remove some ganglia from that region? Will the forward piece move independently of the posterior piece? Benedict Friedländer has made this experiment and found that the coördination continues in spite of the division of the central nervous system (4). If the forward piece begins to move, the aboral piece will also move in the same direction and at the same rate. This overthrows the idea that coördination in these animals is determined by a special centre of coördination which is located in the brain. But how, then, does the coördination take place? When the forward piece elongates and attempts to shorten itself by contracting the longitudinal muscles, the skin of the aboral piece is stretched. This pulling probably acts as a stimulus which causes the longitudinal

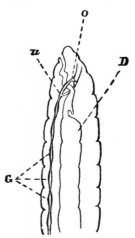

FIG. 28. SIDE VIEW OF THE CENTRAL NERVOUS SYSTEM OF THE EARTHWORM.

o, supracœsophageal ganglion or brain ; *u*, subœsophageal ganglion ; *D*, intestine ; *G*, ganglia of the ventral cord.

muscles of the aboral piece to contract reflexly or perhaps directly. In this way, therefore, coördination between the oral and aboral piece is possible in spite of the interruption of the nervous connection. Friedländer obtained further proof of this by dividing worms completely and connecting the two halves by strings. Even then he found that the aboral piece moved with the anterior piece in a perfectly coördinated way. These facts prove that the brain has no leading rôle in the coördination of the progressive motions of the earthworm.

What part, then, does the central nervous system play in the coördination? It serves only as a quick conductor for the stimuli. Friedländer has shown that the quick motions which an earthworm shows upon a sudden stimulus are no longer transmitted to the posterior part of the body if the ganglion-chain be severed. If the nervous connection be broken so that stimuli cannot be conducted through the nerves, the peripheral structures suffice to make coördinated movement possible.

One might suppose the coördination in the progressive movements of higher animals to be of an entirely different nature from that of worms. An observation made by Goltz, however, shows that in dogs, at least, this is not the case. When a dog with divided spinal cord is lifted up by its fore-legs, so that the back part of the body hangs down perpendicularly, a remarkable phenomenon may be observed. The hind-legs perform pendulum motions which resemble locomotion. These motions are presumably produced by the passive stretching of the skin on the ventral side of the hip-joint by the weight of the legs. These motions are comparable to the reflex contraction of the longitudinal muscles of the earthworm, which is due to the stretching of the skin. Because of this reflex, coördinated locomotion would be quite possible in a dog with divided spinal cord, if the dog only could remain standing on its hind-legs. The walking movement of the fore-legs would cause the stretching which is necessary in order to bring about the walking movement of the hind-legs. The difference in the behaviour of a dog with divided spinal cord and of an earthworm with divided ventral nerve cord in regard to coördinated progressive movements, is not caused so much by differences in the functions of the *central organs* as by differences in the development of the peripheral organs of the skin and of the organs of locomotion. If the dog had short stumps instead of its long, jointed legs, we should have, after dividing the spinal cord, the same phenomenon of progressive movements that we have in the earthworm. The irritability of various parts of the peripheral organs and the simple segmental arrangement of the nervous elements suffice to preserve the locomotion when it has once been started. The correctness of this conclusion is confirmed by experiments on Nereis, which were made in my laboratory by S. S. Maxwell (5). In these animals, the coördination of the movements of the oral and aboral pieces is practically destroyed by dividing the ganglion chain, for the deep incisions between the single segments prevent the entire cutaneous muscle layer from being stretched equally.   The structure of the ventral nerve-cord in Nereis is so similar to that of Lumbricus that we should not be justified in seeking in it for the conditions which cause difference of behaviour.   In earthworms, Maxwell succeeded in confirming Friedländer's observation.   I obtained similar, although not as marked, results on leeches (2).

If an earthworm be divided, the posterior, brainless piece continues to perform progressive movements. This fact confirms the opinion that the brain has no controlling part in progressive movements.

4. The question now arises, Are the remaining characteristic functions of the earthworm brain-functions or segmental functions?   If we place *Lumbricus fœtidus* in a transparent closed vessel, the animals appear to be positively stereotropic.   As soon as they reach an angle in the aquarium, they remain there, crawling along where the glass can touch them on two sides. They are also sensitive to the differences in the intensity of light, remaining in those places where the light is weakest.   It seems, too, when one or more animals settle down anywhere, that the others stop more readily in that place.   This is an illustration of "sociability" among lower animals.   It is probably an instance of chemotropic irritability.   The surface secretions emanating from the worm's body have a quieting influence on other worms of the same kind ;

for this reason they become quiet when in contact with a worm of the same species. These chemical stimuli act as a trap, just as the comparative minimum in the intensity of the light acts. It should be noted, in this connection, that when animals are sensitive to differences in the intensity of light, the less refractive rays which pass through red glass have less effect upon them than the more refractive rays which pass through blue glass. The earthworms become quiet under red glass sooner than under blue glass.

How do decapitated earthworms act? Decapitated *Lumbrici fœtidi* show the same stereotropism that normal worms show. When they reach the concave angle of a vessel, they have no inclination to leave it again. They also show the same response to light. They rest in those places where the intensity of the light is relatively weakest, and they move when the intensity of the light is increased. It can also be shown that light passing through blue glass acts like light of greater intensity, while light passing through red glass has the effect of light of weaker intensity (2).

In all these experiments the decapitated pieces crawl about with either the tail or the anterior end in front.

It is an interesting fact that the reaction-time when light is the stimulus is not appreciably greater in decapitated than in normal earthworms. The animals used for the experiment were in a box in which they could be exposed to diffused daylight suddenly without being jarred. In from three to eighteen seconds after being exposed to the light, the decapitated worms made the first movements. The interval was about the same in normal worms.

Lumbrici fœtidi live in the decaying compost of stables, and probably the chemical nature of certain substances contained in the compost holds them there. When one-half of the bottom of the box is covered with moist white blotting-paper, the other half with a thin layer of compost, all the normal worms that are placed on the paper soon gather on the compost. The aboral pieces of divided worms behave in the same way. When placed upon the blotting-paper, they are not attracted directly by the odours of the compost, but as soon as they come in contact with it in moving about, they crawl on it and do not leave it again. After a short time all the brainless worms are on the compost. When placed on a heap of compost, most of them crawl into it within a short time. This is not due solely to the light, as the same reaction also takes place in the dark (2).

Thus we see that in decapitated earthworms all the reactions shown by the normal worms are retained. Hence the brain (supracœsophageal ganglion) has in this case no leading rôle.

We cannot be too careful in drawing conclusions in regard to the principal function of a ganglion. Nereis, a much more highly developed Annelid than the earthworm, burrows in the sand; if decapitated, this function ceases. One might suspect that this was due to the loss of the brain, but such is not the case.

Earlier experiments had led me to suspect that the
"spontaneous" or "instinctive" burrowing was only
a reflex produced by the contact-stimuli of the sand.
I then attempted to find out whether it were not possible under special conditions to produce the same
reflex in brainless pieces. I placed such a piece of a
Nereis on the sand ; as usual it remained quiet. I
then gradually covered the forward end with sand.
The rest of the animal immediately began to make
the typical movements which the animal makes in
forcing its way into the sand. At the same time the
glands began to secrete the sticky substance which
cements the particles of sand together, forming the
wall of the burrow-hole. This secretion-phenomenon
regularly accompanies the burrowing of these animals ;
it is the same secretion that in other animals leads to
the formation of a case.

But why does the Nereis not burrow when deprived
of its brain ? For the simple reason that it makes
use of the organs of the mouth in burrowing, and these
are amputated with the head. Hence it is the loss of
a peripheral head-organ which keeps the decapitated
Nereis from burrowing, and not the loss of the brain.
The brain in this case merely performs the function
of a segmental ganglion—that is, it acts as the ganglion
of that segment to which the peripheral head-organ
belongs.

5. We will now turn our attention to the brain-
functions of Nereis.

After a Nereis has burrowed in the sand it lives in

the same case for a long time. If the supraœsophageal ganglion (*o*, Fig. 26) be removed, the animal becomes restless, as S. S. Maxwell has found. It crawls about on the sand unceasingly, making no attempt to burrow. This restlessness is marked by one feature which we find in higher animals after certain injuries to the brain — namely, the Nereis does not withdraw from obstacles but attempts to force its way through them.

If normal Nereis are in a square aquarium the bottom of which is covered with sand, they will crawl about, if undisturbed, on the sides of the glass. This is the result of stereotropism. A Nereis that has lost the supraœsophageal ganglion will behave in the same way, except that when it reaches a corner it does not turn out but attempts to go through the glass. If there are several animals which have been operated upon in a vessel, they will assume the position represented in Fig. 29. The worms remained like this for many hours at a time, and then died in consequence of their vain attempt to go forward. Those reactions are wanting which in the normal Nereis result from the application of contact-stimuli to the oral end. The reader who is familiar with brain-physiology may already have been reminded in this connection of the dogs from which Goltz removed the anterior half of the cerebral hemispheres.

If glass tubes 20 cm. long, with a bore a little larger than the diameter of the worm, are placed in an aquarium without sand, the normal Nereis will

crawl into them and will not leave them again.   This
is due to stereotropism.   If there are, for instance,
six such tubes in a vessel and six normal Nereis are
put into it, we may be sure that after a few hours
every Nereis will have established itself in a tube.   It

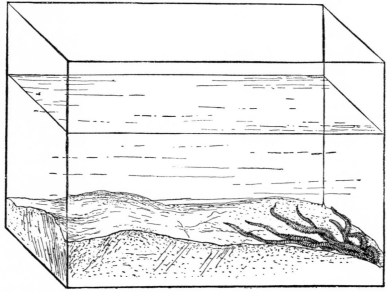

FIG. 29.   A GROUP OF NEREIS WHOSE BRAINS HAVE BEEN REMOVED.   THEY AT
LAST COLLECT IN A CORNER OF THE AQUARIUM AND PERISH IN THEIR VAIN
ATTEMPT TO GO THROUGH THE GLASS.   (After Maxwell.)

frequently occurs that a Nereis goes into a tube that
already has an occupant.   In that case the new-comer
withdraws with a start as soon as it touches the old
occupant.   As long as the new-comer is in possession of its brain, it leaves the tube under such

circumstances, but if it has lost the supraœsophageal ganglion, the presence of the other worm in the tube has no inhibitory effect. It tries to force its way into the tube even if it perishes in the attempt. If both worms have lost the supraœsophageal ganglion, they rub their heads together until they are sore. If we wish to keep them alive, they must be separated by breaking the tube. If we compare the conduct of a Nereis whose brain has been amputated, with that of a normal worm, the difference seems to be of the same nature as that between an insane and a rational human being. It would be erroneous, however, to conclude that the normal, brain-endowed Nereis possesses reason or intelligence. The peculiar irritability by means of which the Nereis draws its head back and moves backward out of the tube depends upon organs which are located in the forward end of the body and whose sensory nerves go to the supraœsophageal ganglion. Hence, if the supraœsophageal ganglion is extirpated, the connection between these organs and the rest of the body is interrupted, and the stimuli which affect the forward part of the body can no longer produce backward movements in the posterior portion of the animal.

This does not, however, explain the change of character, the restlessness of the Nereis which has been deprived of its brain. It is maintained that, if the spontaneous activity or the reflex irritability of an animal is increased after the loss of a part of the brain, that part is an inhibitory mechanism. Nothing is gained, however, by making such a statement. We wish to know *how* the supracœsophageal ganglion can inhibit movements, and how its absence can increase spontaneity.

It is not possible to offer at present more than a suggestion. We can increase and decrease the loco-motor activity of a jelly-fish at desire by changing the constitution of the sea-water. If we increase the number of Na ions in the sea-water, the rate of rhythmical contractions in Gonionemus increases and the animal becomes restless. If the number of Ca ions be increased, the animal becomes quiet. It is, moreover, a fact that the different parts of a Gonionemus are affected somewhat differently by the same ions, inasmuch as the margin is more immune against the effects of Ca ions than the centre. I think it possible that there is a similar difference between the segments belonging to the supracœsophageal and subœsophageal ganglion. It might be possible that the ions (or some other substance) of the blood influence the supracœsophageal ganglion or its segments in such a way as to cause a decrease in the locomotions, while the same constituents of the blood do not have such an effect upon the subœsophageal ganglion or its segment. But the blood is not the only agency which is to be considered in this connection. The supraœsophageal ganglion of Annelids is connected with the alimentary canal by nerves. The processes which go on in the intestine—that is, the chemical pro-cesses of secretion and digestion—can only affect the whole animal nervously as long as the supraœsopha-geal ganglion is intact. If it is removed, the whole influence of this so-called sympathetic nervous system ceases. It is possible that the stimuli which pass from the sympathetic into the central nervous system may condition the alternation of rest and activity which characterises the normal animal, and that the removal of this stimulation may remove the necessity of resting.

Maxwell has found that a Nereis which has lost the subœsophageal ganglion becomes quiet. Such ani-mals make no attempt at burrowing. The reason for this is that the motor nerves of the œsophageal mus-cles originate in the subœsophageal ganglion, so that removal of this ganglion causes paresis or paralysis of these muscles. The pharynx plays a great rôle in bor-ing the hole. It is due to this same paralysis or paresis of the œsophageal muscles that a Nereis no longer eats after losing the subœsophageal ganglion (5).

We wish to mention here, however, that removal of the subœsophageal ganglion does not bring about disturbances in taking up food in *all* Annelids. Max-well found that the leech is still able to suck itself full of blood after losing the ganglion. McCaskill dis-covered, however, that in the leech the motor nerves of the sucking apparatus originate in the supra-œsophageal ganglion. The subœsophageal ganglion in the leech behaves like the first link in the ganglion-chain.

As regards the restlessness of Nereis after removal

of the supraœsophageal ganglion and the repose after the removal of the subœsophageal ganglion, we wish to emphasise the fact that they have nothing to do with the wound. Maxwell's observations were made on animals whose wounds were healed. If we make a wound like that made in removing the ganglion, only with the difference that the ganglion is left intact, none of the above-mentioned disturbances occur. Immediately after the operation the worm burrows again in spite of the wound.

Differences like those found between the behaviour of normal Nereis and of Nereis from which the brain has been removed do not appear in earthworms under the same conditions. What causes this difference? Is the supraœsophageal ganglion in the earthworm a segmental ganglion, while in Nereis it is a "controlling ganglion," a brain in the sense of the anthropomorphic nerve-physiology?

I am inclined to believe that we have to deal with differences of the same character as those found between Acalephæ and Hydromedusæ. In addition it should be said that there is a much higher degree of differentiation of the head-organs in Nereis than in the earthworm. We have already seen in preceding chapters that the apparent functions of the brain or of the ganglia are chiefly determined by the peripheral organs. In Nereis the differentiation of the head-segments is carried much farther than that of the other segments (Fig. 30). In the earthworm, on the other hand, the difference is much less (Fig. 27).

7

In Vertebrates the head contains special sense-organs, mouth-organs, which are lacking in the other segments. In judging of the relation of the brain-ganglia to the other segmental ganglia of the body this fact should not be overlooked. Not infrequently physiologists have ascribed to a ganglion what in reality was due to the higher differentiation of the peripheral organs of the segment.

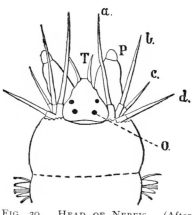

FIG. 30.   HEAD OF NEREIS.   (After Quatrefages.)

We desire now to touch briefly upon the behaviour of the muscles after extirpation of the ganglion, for the phenomena will occupy our attention repeatedly.

In the case of loss or a congenital lack of a piece of the spinal cord, the skeletal muscles belonging to the corresponding segment atrophy. Nothing of the kind occurs in leeches or earthworms from whose ventral chain a piece has been removed. I believe that the difference is determined as follows : In worms direct impulses flow from the neighbouring muscles to the muscles that have been deprived of their ganglion, while in Vertebrates, as soon as the spinal cord is destroyed, the protoplasmic connection between the skeletal muscles and the rest of the body is destroyed and it is not possible for stimuli to be transmitted. In the muscles of the blood-vessels of the Vertebrates, however, a conduction of the stimulation from element to element is possible. For this reason their reactions remain intact even in higher animals after destruction of the corresponding segments of the spinal cord. In Nereis, after division of the ganglion-chain, a phenomenon may be observed that reminds one of the Brondgeestian phenomenon. The back part of the body becomes more flat, while the part that is connected with the brain remains round. This indicates a relaxation of the ring-muscles in the part of the animal that is situated behind the point of division.

The results of our physiological analysis of the functions of the central nervous system in Annelids are in perfect harmony with Professor C. O. Whitman's investigations on the morphological structure of the central nervous system in Annelids. He arrives at the conclusion that the brain of Annelids is not of a higher order than the other segmental ganglia (7).

BIBLIOGRAPHY.

1. LANG, A. *Untersuchungen zur vergleichenden Anatomie und Histologie des Nervensystems der Plathelminthen. Mittheil. aus der Zoolog. Station zu Neapel*, Bd. I.

2. LOEB, J. *Beiträge zur Gehirnphysiologie der Würmer, Pflüger's Archiv*, Bd. 56, 1894 ; and *Ueber künstliche Umwandlung positiv helistropischer Thiere in negativ heliotropische und umgekehrt, Pflüger's Archiv*, Bd. 54, 1893.

3. GRABER. *Grundlinien zur Erforschung des Helligkeits-und*

Farbensinns der Thiere. Prag und Leipzig, 1884. Verlag von Tempsky & Freitag.

4. FRIEDLÄNDER, BENEDICT. *Ueber das Kriechen der Regenwürmer, Biologisches Centralblatt,* Bd. 8 ; and *Zur Beurtheilung und Erforschung der thierischen Bewegungen, Biolog. Centralblatt,* Bd. 11 ; and *Beiträge zur Physiologie des Centralnervensystems und des Bewegungsmechanismus der Regenwürmer, Pflüger's Archiv,* Bd. 58.

5. MAXWELL, S. S. *Beiträge zur Gehirnphysiologie der Anneliden. Pflüger's Archiv,* Bd. 67, 1897.

6. VAN DUYNE, JOHN. *Ueber Heteromorphose bei Planarien. Pflüger's Archiv,* Bd. 64, 1897.

7. WHITMAN, C. O. *The Metamerism of Clepsine. Festschrift für Leuckart,* Leipzig, 1892.

CHAPTER VII

EXPERIMENTS ON ARTHROPODS

1. Experiments on the lowest animal forms have taught us that the peculiar reactions of animals are determined, first, by the different forms of irritability of the elements composing the tissues, and, second, by the arrangement of the muscle-fibres. The central nervous system does not control response to stimulation : it merely serves as a conductor from the point of stimulation to the muscle through which weaker stimuli may pass, and pass more rapidly than would be possible if the muscle were stimulated directly.

In the Annelids each ganglion is the relay station for the sensory and motor nerves of the corresponding segment. If the head exercises a stronger influence upon the behaviour of the animal than any other segment, as in Nereis, for instance, I believe it is due to the fact that in the oral end more kinds of irritability are present and more peripheral organs are differentiated (sense-organs, mouth, etc.) than in the other segments. The fact that in this case the sympathetic nervous system takes its origin from the supraœsophageal ganglion also helps to increase the predominance of the head-segments. Hence it is not the presence of the supraœsophageal ganglion which determines the greater number of reactions and their more complicated nature in the oral segments of some Annelids, but it is the presence of the greater number of irritabilities and the greater number of specific organs in the forward end of the body. In addition there may exist chemical differences between the various segments of an animal.

We shall now see that this conception of the central nervous system also holds good for the Arthropods. We will begin the analysis of the brain-functions of these forms with *Limulus polyphemus* (Fig. 31).

Zoölogists maintain that Limulus is a very old form. If tenacity of life favours the age of the species as it does the age of individuals, this assertion can be readily understood, for it is difficult to conceive of a tougher animal. At my suggestion, Miss Ida Hyde made experiments on the functions of the single parts of the central nervous system of *Limulus polyphemus*, with special attention to the respiratory centres (1). Concerning these centres, Faivre had made assertions which did not harmonise with the apparent segmental arrangement of the central nervous system. He assumes that the subœsophageal ganglion which is located in the head has a coördinating influence on the respiratory movements, but in forms like these with the respiratory organs (gills) in the abdomen, the respiratory nerves must originate in the abdominal ganglion-chain. The conditions existing in Verte-

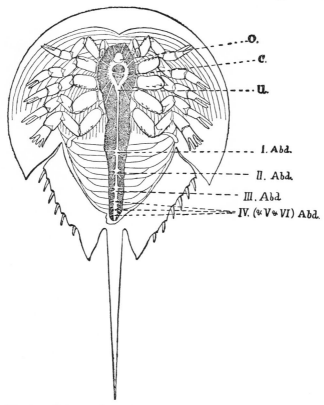

FIG. 31. LIMULUS POLYPHEMUS WITH THE CENTRAL NERVOUS SYSTEM EXPOSED.

o, supraœsophageal ganglion ; *c*, commissure ; *u*, subœsophageal ganglion ; *I–IV* (*V and VI Abd.*), abdominal ganglia of the respiratory segments.

brates evidently gave rise to the idea of a coördinating ganglion located in the head. In Vertebrates the diaphragm, the chief respiratory muscle, is far separated from its nervous segment, but this is due merely to a shifting during development. The Anlage is really located near the head. Such displacements during growth do not take place to this extent in Arthropods. Faivre seems to have been entirely under the influence of current views of Vertebrate physiology, especially those of Flourens, and so he was led into making incorrect statements regarding the physiology of the invertebrates.

The central nervous system of Limulus consists of the following parts (Fig. 31) : A supracœsophageal ganglion *o*, which is usually called the brain, an œsophageal ring (*c*, Fig. 31) which encloses the œsophagus and consists of fibres and ganglia, a sub-œsophageal ganglion *u*, and the ventral chain with six abdominal ganglia. These parts send out a series of peripheral nerves. In Limulus the situation of the nerve-centres is schematically developed : every peripheral organ has its nerve-centre in that part of the nervous system which belongs to its segment. Perhaps this can be best seen from the following experiment made by Miss Hyde : The whole central nervous system of a Limulus was removed with the exception of a little piece of the œsophagus-ring (*c*, Fig. 31) and the abdominal ganglia (I–VI *Abd*, Fig. 31). No connection remained between these two pieces. The piece of the œsophageal ring lay at the same height with the three mouth-appendages that are used for taking in food. These three mouth-appendages retained their function, and eating movements were performed reflexly when meat was placed on the appendages. The rest of the appendages were entirely paralysed, with the exception of the gills on the ventral side of the abdomen. The animal was reduced to a mere eating and breathing machine. It was fed artificially and so kept alive.

Patten has shown further that each feeding-appendage continues to take food normally and carries it to the mouth if the piece of the œsophagus-ring from which its nerves take their origin is preserved. These feeding-appendages discriminate the chemical and tactile nature of the food that is offered them, just as the tentacles of the Actinians do—they refuse to accept it unless the substances offered fulfil certain chemical and mechanical conditions. As regards the conception of these phenomena and their mechanics, no difference, of course, exists between the behaviour of the tentacles of the Actinians and the behaviour of the mouth-appendages of the Limuli except that determined by the skeletal relations.

If we remove one half (for instance, the right half) of the supraœsophageal ganglion in Limulus (*o*, Fig. 31), the animal usually moves no longer straight ahead, but in a circle with more or less of a curvature toward the uninjured (left) side. This is an instance of the well-known circus-motions. We shall return to the mechanics of such motions in a later chapter.

If the whole supraœsophageal ganglion be removed, the animal is able to take food placed upon the mouth-organs, but loses its spontaneity in so far as this is expressed by progressive movements. It will even retain abnormal postures in which it is placed. The operations were performed during the period of heat. Male Limuli that had lost the supra-œsophageal ganglion no longer noticed the females. On the other hand, the legs attempted to remove an irritating object from the surface of the body. De-capitated frogs act in the same way.

In the cases mentioned above, the Limuli had en-dured the operation well and their wounds were entirely healed. If the œsophageal commissure (*c*, Fig. 31) be severed on one side, circus-movements will appear in the direction of the injured side, but these only last until the wound is healed. The circus-motions which ensue upon extirpation of one-half of the brain also disappear after a time. If ganglia be removed from the œsophagus-ring, the appendages corresponding to the extirpated ganglia are perma-nently paralysed.

2. After extirpation of the subœsophageal ganglion (*u*, Fig. 31) the animal remains extremely quiet, and often lies on the same spot for days. But its respira-tion continues normal, and this proves the erroneous-ness of Faivre's opposed assertion. Except for its immobility and the fact that the extensors of the joint between the thorax and abdomen are paralysed as a result of nerve-injuries, the animal appears normal.

The four or six ganglia of the abdomen (Fig. 31)

innervate the five gills which are located on the abdomen of the animal. If the whole central nervous system with the exception of these ganglia be removed, the rhythmical respiratory activity continues unchanged. Immediately after the operation, which is accompanied by a great loss of blood, the respiration may be interrupted for an hour or more. If we touch the gill-plates during this time, the stimulation occasions a series of rhythmical respiratory movements which, however, soon cease. After a time, the gills begin their respiratory activity again spontaneously, and are only interrupted by an occasional cramp. This interruption of the respiratory movements is also found occasionally in the normal Limulus, where, if it remains quiet, the respiratory movements may cease for an hour or more. At this place we will not go into details concerning this phenomenon.

The abdominal ganglia are thus centres for the automatic movements of the abdominal gill-plates. All the gills move in the same phase. It is probable that the inspiration begins with the first gill and extends to the following gills in succession, but rapidly enough to make the whole appear simultaneous. According to the prevailing opinions, we should be obliged to assume from this either that only one, for instance the first, of the four abdominal ganglia, is automatically active, and that the rest are stimulated from this, or that, if each of the four ganglia is rhythmically active, a common centre of coördination exists somewhere in the four ganglia. If we sever the ventral cord between two ganglia, for instance between the second and third, we find that in spite of the division all the gills continue to breathe. Any ganglion may be entirely isolated—that is, the commissure before and behind it may be severed, and the corresponding gill continue to make respiratory motions. This proves that *every ganglion* is the seat of an automatic periodic activity. But how does it happen that all the gills move simultaneously as long as their ganglia are connected? The number of the respirations produced is the same even when the abdominal ganglia are isolated. This is probably due to the fact that the number of respirations is determined by the temperature and the chemical nature of the blood. The amount of carbon dioxide and certain other substances, especially those formed in the muscles (Zuntz and Geppert), controls the number of respirations. The phase of the movement, on the other hand, is not the same in the various segments where the ganglia are isolated. The gills that are situated anterior to the place of incision may be inspiring while those behind the incision are expiring. These phenomena lead me to believe that in the normal animal coördination is regulated in the same way that it is regulated in the activity of the heart and in the movements of Medusæ. The ganglion that acts first, that is to say, the ganglion that acts quickest, stimulates those connected with it nervously and so determines the correspondence of phase. This view is supported by the fact that no matter how the ganglia may be separated from each other, those that are connected nervously always keep their gills in the same phase of activity. Were there a centre of coördination in any ganglion, a group of ganglia separated from this centre would be active in an uncoördinated manner, but such is never the case.

3. In higher animals, the conditions controlling respiration scarcely differ from those in Limulus. There is a series of segmental ganglia in the thoracic portion of the spinal cord which sends nerves to the thoracic respiratory muscles of the respective segments. These ganglia extend into the cervical portion of the spinal cord, and the fourth, third, and fifth pairs of spinal nerves give rise to the fibres of the phrenic nerve which goes to the diaphragm. The diaphragm in reality belongs to the corresponding segments of the neck portion, and has attained its present position only through a shifting of position during growth. One would expect in text-books of physiology to find the phenomena of respiration explained as follows: Chemical changes which are continually going on in the body, or in these segmental ganglia, under the influence of heat (the temperature of the body), produce a periodic activity in these ganglia and consequently in the respiratory muscles. The segmental connection existing between the ganglia and the muscles would bring about coördination just as it does in Limulus. But in the majority of text-books we find statements of the following character: The automatic activity of the respiratory muscles is pro-

duced much higher up, at a certain point of the medulla oblongata near the place where the vagus enters, which Flourens called the nœud vital. This place is supposed to be the respiratory centre. This view is justified by two facts : first, the destruction of the nœud vital causes a cessation of respiration ; and, second, severing the spinal cord between the nœud vital and the origin of the phrenic nerve likewise causes respiration to cease. These facts do not justify the conclusion that Le Gallois, Flourens, and with him the majority of modern physiologists, have drawn — namely, that the automatic activity of respiration is located not in the segmental ganglia, but higher up in the nœud vital. We should have just as much right to assume that in Limulus the rhythmical respiratory activity was produced higher up, in the subœsophageal ganglion for instance, for in this animal, too, respiration ceases for a time immediately after the removal of the subœsophageal ganglion. We have seen in this case, however, that the cessation is only temporary, and is due to the shock, for respiratory activity can go on again even when the whole central nervous system, with the exception of the abdominal ganglia, has been removed. Neither is the cessation of respiration in Vertebrates permanent after removal of the nœud vital or division of the spinal cord between the nœud vital and the third cervical vertebra. Langendorff has made the important discovery that decapitated Vertebrates which have lost the nœud vital are still able to perform independent respiratory

movements (2). It was necessary to make these experiments on young or new-born Vertebrates, as on them
the effect of the shock does not last so long. If one
succeeds in keeping these animals alive by introducing
artificial respiration until the effect of the shock resulting from the operation has passed off, spontaneous
respiration begins again. I consider it possible that,
if we could keep an adult Vertebrate alive without the
nœud vital for some time, the respiratory motions
would be resumed again. But why does respiration
stop temporarily after the isolation of the segmental respiratory ganglia from the higher parts of the central
nervous system? An answer to this question would be
in part an explanation of the mystery of the shock-
effects. It might be possible that something has to be
supplied constantly by certain nerve-elements in the
subœsophageal ganglion or the medulla to the segmental respiratory ganglia, which enables the latter to
be active automatically. In destroying the nœud vital
we perhaps destroy the pathway along which these
constant impulses are carried to the segmental respiratory ganglia in the spinal cord. But where do
these impulses come from and what is their character?
In watching the respiratory motions of a Limulus, I
received the impression that the operculum always
moves first, and that the respiratory motions of the
lower segments follow successively. In the lower
Vertebrates, *e. g.* the frog, we have a mouth respiration, whose segmental ganglia are situated in the
medulla. Likewise the segmental ganglia for the

respiratory activity of the gills in fish are situated in the medulla. Could it not be possible that in Mammalians the segmental ganglia for the gill-respiration continue to be active, although the gills or the oral respiration have disappeared? If this were so, we can understand that the segmental ganglia for gill-respiration in the medulla begin to be active first. Their activity is the stimulus for the activity of the next lower segmental ganglion, and so on.

If we cut the cord between medulla and phrenic nerve, respiration must stop. But if we could keep such an animal alive long enough, the lower segmental ganglia would be altered in such a way as to breathe automatically again.

That the shock-effect after such an operation cannot be due to an exhaustion of the phrenic ganglia is made obvious by the following experiment: W. T. Porter made hemisections of the spinal cord between the medulla oblongata and the origin of the phrenic nerves (3). If one half, for instance the left half, of the medulla be cut, the left half of the diaphragm no longer partakes in the respiratory movements, while the respiratory motions of the right half continue. But if the right phrenic be cut, the left half of the diaphragm begins its rhythmical motion again, while the right half of the diaphragm stops breathing. It is of course, at present, just as impossible to explain why the cutting of the right phrenic nerve causes the left half of the diaphragm to breathe again, as it is to explain why a frog that had lost its spontaneity after an operation in the thalamus opticus begins to move spontaneously again if the optic lobes and the pars commissuralis of the medulla are removed.

In Limulus an anterior and a posterior nerve originate from every ganglion of the ventral chain. It was interesting to determine whether these nerves have functional differences like those of the anterior and posterior roots of the spinal cord of Vertebrates. It has been maintained that Arthropods are Vertebrates that walk on their backs. Faivre has stated that there is not only a separation of the motor and sensory roots in Arthropods, corresponding to Bell's law, but that also in Arthropods, in contrast with Vertebrates, the ventral side of the ganglia is sensory, the dorsal motor. Now this is not true of the nerve-roots which start from the ganglia in Limulus. If the posterior nerve be severed and its peripheral stump stimulated, we get inspiratory movements of the half of the gills to which this nerve goes. All the other gills are unaffected. Hence this nerve contains motor fibres. If the ventral stump be stimulated, the whole animal becomes much excited. From this we see that the posterior nerve also contains sensory fibres. If the anterior nerve be severed, stimulation of the peripheral stump has no effect. Stimulation of the central stump excites the entire animal. Hence the anterior nerve is purely sensory. Limulus is better adapted for deciding this question than the smaller Arthropods. The conditions in the latter are probably the same as in the former, for Vulpian (4) and latterly Bethe (5) energetically reject the idea that dorso-ventrally the ganglion-chain of Arthropods is the reverse of the spinal cord of Vertebrates.

4. We will now turn our attention to the crayfish as the next representative of the Arthropods whose brain-physiology has been carefully investigated. Fig. 32 gives a diagram of the central nervous system of the lobster, which is almost identical with that of the crayfish. *o* is the supracesophageal ganglion with the nerves for the eyes and antennæ. In addition it gives off the sympathetic nervous system which goes to the intestine. Both œsophageal commissures, *c*, go backwards to the subœsophageal ganglion, *u*. The latter is seemingly one ganglion, but it supplies six pairs of segmental organs, namely, the mouth-appendages. The microscopical examination shows that this subœsophageal ganglion in reality consists of six separate ganglia. We often meet with a fusion of ganglia, and consequently an apparent lack of clearness in the segmental arrangement. It is due to this fact that in the brain-physiology of Vertebrates the segmental arrangement of the central nervous system has been left entirely out of consideration. Next after the subœsophageal ganglion come the five thoracic ganglia (I–V *T*, Fig. 32) belonging to the segments of the forceps and the four pairs of loco-motor appendages. In addition to these, there are the five ganglia of the abdomen (I-V *Abd.*, Fig. 32) that innervate the swimmerets, and the tail, which serves as a swimming-organ. The best experiments

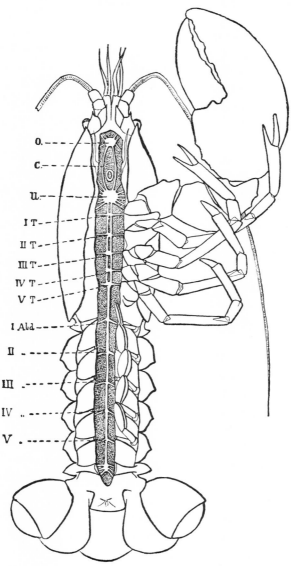

FIG. 32. LOBSTER WITH CENTRAL NERVOUS SYSTEM
EXPOSED.

o, supraœsophageal ganglion (brain) ; *c*, commissure ; *u*, subœsophageal
ganglion ; *I–V T*, five thoracic ganglia ; *I–V Abd.*, first five abdominal
ganglia.

on the central nervous system of these animals have unquestionably been made by Bethe, and we shall in the main follow his presentation. Many of the facts which Bethe describes from the animals used in his experiments are familiar to me from personal observation, and I am convinced that the picture he gives is correct.

If in a crayfish both the commissures (c, Fig. 32) which connect the supraœsophageal ganglion o with the rest of the brain be severed, the behaviour of the animal is no longer controlled by the brain o. It does not make spontaneous progressive movements. When stimulated it begins to move, but after having gone about 20 cm. it stops. This lack of spontaneous progressive movements agrees with the description given by Flourens of the Vertebrate from which the cerebral hemispheres had been removed. Flourens's representation was wrong, however, for a dog operated upon in this way shows increased spontaneity in its progressive movements.

Annelids and Arthropods are closely related as regards the central nervous system. However, Nereis shows an excess of progressive movements after removal of the supraœsophageal ganglion, while Astacus no longer moves spontaneously. I believe that the difference depends only upon circumstances of minor importance. Ward has already found—and Bethe has confirmed the fact—that in brainless crayfish the legs are unceasingly active, either cleaning each other or performing pendulum-movements.

They, however, make no progressive movements. I believe this is due possibly to a secondary effect of the extirpation of the supracœsophageal ganglion. The legs of such an animal have an abnormal position, being more strongly flexed at the joints nearest the body than they are normally. The tension of the extensors probably suffered severely from the operation. Such mechanical disturbances might easily cause difficulty in locomotion, while simple pendulum-movements of the legs, which require practically no labor, could still be performed. The fact that after removal of the brain of crayfish the tension of the flexors predominates in certain joints is of interest, as we meet with the same phenomenon in dogs that have lost the anterior region of the cerebral hemispheres, and as it also comes to our attention in man after apoplexies which result in the paralysis of an arm.

Bethe concludes from these pendulum-movements that the brain is an organ of inhibition. As regards this, the remarks hold good that have already been made in this connection on annelids (see p. 94).

The weakening of the muscles in the crayfish whose brain has been extirpated shows itself also in the fact that the forceps no longer pinch as hard as those of normal animals.

After what has been said concerning the segmental character of the central nervous system, it is to be expected in the crayfish that, since the segmental ganglia of the organs of mastication are located in the subœsophageal ganglion, extirpation of the supraœsophageal ganglion will not interfere with the normal character of its eating movements. I give the description in Bethe's words : " The animal devoid of the supraœsophageal ganglion is able to eat and selects its food. It is true that pebbles, small pieces of wood, etc., are seized by the forceps of the front pairs of legs, but when brought near the mouth they are rejected. A piece of meat, however, is always taken into the mouth and masticated. The swallowing is difficult, just as in the case of Carcinus. The piece often remains for a long time between the maxillipedes without being swallowed, and at last falls to the ground. Pieces of paper that have been saturated with meat-juice are treated in the same way. Stones that have been covered with meat-juice are also brought to the mouth, but no attempt is made to masticate them. They are usually dropped as soon as they come in contact with the maxillipedes." Thus we see that the nature of the stimulus determines the results just as in the case of Actinians. The brain of the crayfish has nothing to do with these reactions. The central nervous system is in this case to be considered only as an organ for the conduction of stimuli, a function that could just as well be performed by plant protoplasm or muscle-tissue as by nerve-protoplasm. In the crayfish, the original segmental arrangement of the nervous elements is so well preserved that removal of the brain does not interrupt the protoplasmic nervous connection between the surface of the mouth and the muscles of the thoracic appendages.

When these animals from which the brain has been removed are laid on their backs they return to the ventral position.

The observations made by Bethe in crayfish in which he had severed the œsophageal commissures on only one side are interesting. The division was made on the right side. If he touched the left side of the head of such an animal, first the forceps of the stimulated side reached toward the stimulated spot and then those of the other side followed with accuracy. At the same time, the animal attempted to escape backwards. If the same stimulus was applied to the right side of the head, the forceps did not react. Even with a strong stimulus no reaction followed. Hence the stimulus that produces the localising reflex can only be transmitted through the longitudinal commissure of the same side to the appendages. This seems to hold good generally for the Arthropods, since Bethe was able to prove it in Carcinus, Squilla, and Hydrophylus. It seems to hold good not only for the conduction through the œsophageal commissures but through all longitudinal commissures. After division of an œsophageal commissure, circus-motions often but not always occur toward the normal side. The animal is also able to move straight ahead, but this requires some effort.

If the right œsophageal commissure be severed, the tonus of the muscles on the right side (the injured side) of the abdomen is diminished, and as a result the abdomen is curved toward the left and becomes concave on that side.

Division of the brain in the middle line—that is, separation of the two halves of the brain—destroys the geotropic reactions of the eyestalks. It is still more remarkable that such animals no longer prefer to remain in the dark like normal animals.

If the longitudinal commissures be divided between the mouth-ganglia (suboesophageal ganglion) and the ganglion of the chelæ, all locomotor movements become impossible, although the legs are not paralysed. This is strange, because the suboesophageal ganglion contains the segmental nerve-elements of the oral appendages but not those of the locomotor appendages. In other Crustaceans, extirpation of the suboesophageal ganglion has no such paralysing effect on the locomotor movements. It is impossible to tell at present what causes the exceptional behaviour of Astacus in this regard. I do not believe we are obliged to assume that this is an instance of a deviation from the laws of the segmental arrangement of the nerve-elements (centres) of the limbs. This is shown by the fact that the legs of such an animal are not paralysed, but are unceasingly occupied in cleaning the abdomen, the pedes spurii, or each other. Indeed, more than that, "if we give one of the forceps of a locomotor appendage a piece of meat or paper, other legs approach immediately, seize the meat, and carry it to the mouth," in spite of the fact that all nervous connection between the nerves of the mouth-organs and the legs has been severed. It is true that the appendages around the mouth often refuse to accept and forward the pieces of meat that are thus offered them by the legs.

As regards the further isolation of the ganglia that are located posterior to the subœsophageal ganglion, the facts which have been described in Limulus are in general true. As long as the ganglion of a segment remains connected with the segmental organs, the functions of that segment remain unimpaired. Bethe has found single exceptions to this rule, but it is conceivable that these exceptions are shock-effects resulting from the operation.

We will now report more briefly concerning Bethe's experiments on some other Arthropods.

5. Squilla no longer swims spontaneously after the supraœsophageal ganglion has been isolated (that is, after division of the commissure between the supraœsophageal ganglion and the mouth-ganglion). The spontaneous progressive movements usually seem to be destroyed. When stimulated, however, the animal moves normally. The nervous mechanism for the locomotor reflexes is localised in the three ganglia of the locomotor appendages, that is, these appendages still move normally, even though the connection with the ganglia lying in front has been interrupted.

In grasshoppers (*Pachytylus cinerascens*) isolation of the supraœsophageal ganglion causes the spontaneous progressive movements to cease. These animals, after the operation, clean their antennæ with their fore-legs like a normal animal. According to Bethe these localised reflexes of the legs are produced by the stimulus of the operation. Abnormal positions of the legs, resulting from the operation, occur just as in Astacus and Squilla.

If the supra- and subœsophageal ganglia be removed by decapitating the animals, they are still able to perform some walking movements, and especially hopping movements, when stimulated. This agrees with the idea of the preservation of the purely segmental arrangement of the nerve-connections. Yersin's experiments on crickets are very significant in this regard. I take them from Bethe's paper. They deal with crickets from which both longitudinal commissures had been removed between the subœsophageal ganglion and the first thoracic ganglion. Yersin kept these animals alive for weeks. "When laid on their backs they were able to turn over. When stimulated they moved forward a few steps, or to the side, according to the point of stimulation. In doing so they occasionally tumbled over. When stimulated, they still made attempts at flying without being able to lift themselves from the ground." Yersin observed that a male and a female, both of which had been operated upon in this way, were able to pair. Of course it was necessary to place the male on the female in this case. The male on which he made this observation had already given off a spermatophore.

Bees lived only a short time after the extirpation of the supraœsophageal ganglion. The bee shows the same restlessness that was noticed in Astacus.

Bees whose brains were divided lengthwise in

symmetrical halves showed a perceptible functional disorder only in their behaviour toward the hive. " If carried back to it they crawl about on the board before the entrance but make no attempt to enter, and they pay no attention to their companions."

If bees be decapitated, the supra- and subœsophageal ganglion being thus removed, they are still able to walk, although awkwardly. When laid on their backs they turn over with the help of their legs. " When stimulated on the ventral side they grasp the object (pencil) with their legs, pull it toward them, bend the abdomen, and attempt to sting it." But not all animals give such favourable results. In brain-physiology only those animals operated upon which show the slightest disorders can be considered, because the exhaustion may render the rest of the central nervous system pathological.

As was to be expected *a priori* on the basis of the segmental theory, the stinging-reflex is possible as long as the abdominal ganglion is preserved. Bethe showed that the abdomen, when severed from the body, still bends if stimulated on the ventral side and reaches the stimulated spot with the outstretched sting. At the same time poison is ejected. The reflex also continues when all the abdominal segments with the exception of the last one have been amputated.

If the supraœsophageal ganglion in a water-beetle (Hydrophilus) be extirpated, *the progressive locomotor movements are not only not interrupted, but the animal goes about almost unceasingly*, showing only modifications which suggest that the relation in the tension of the antagonistic muscles of its legs is changed. The animal turns out for obstacles that come in its way. If a beetle that has lost the supracœsophageal ganglion is thrown into water it swims off, drawing in the first pair of legs. The normal water-beetle rests quietly under dark objects. The water-beetle whose supracœsophageal ganglion has been divided by a longitudinal incision no longer shows these reactions, although the light is still able to produce other effects in the animal. If suddenly exposed to strong light or a dark shadow—when in motion, namely—it ceases to move.

An animal whose right œsophageal commissure has been severed does not brace itself against obstacles as strongly with the legs of the right side as with those of the left side. It seems to me this shows that the extensors of the right side are weakened, as it is they that have to perform the task of bracing. Furthermore, the right legs are moved constantly. It may be possible that these two facts are in some way connected. The decreased opposition of the extensors renders the pendulum-movements of the legs easier. The same explanation may hold for Astacus, bees, etc. If the supra- and subœsophageal ganglia be extirpated, the animal only makes progressive movements when stimulated. But the ability to perform coördinated progressive movements is not destroyed. When laid on its back the animal still tries to regain the ventral position, but the efforts made by the legs are vain.

If put under water it still makes swimming movements, but these do not help it forward.

The experiments on the other ganglia of this animal performed by Bethe do not concern us in this book. We will only quote that result of Bethe's which is of most importance for our purpose: " Neither the suboesophageal nor the prothoracic ganglion is the seat of the reflex for righting the animal when turned on its back, nor of the coördination of the muscles of locomotion, walking, or swimming, as Faivre maintains. It would seem as though *these reflexes were located rather in each thoracic ganglion for the corresponding segment.*" This last sentence expresses the principal truth for all complicated central nervous systems. Each segment of a segmented animal may be regarded as a simple reflex animal, comparable to the Ascidian, and the analysis of the reflexes depends upon the same principles and leads to the same results in both cases. The complication that appears in segmented animals consists in the fact that when a process of stimulation takes place in one segment it is communicated to the neighbouring ganglia, and these ganglia produce processes of the same kind. It is possible that the nature of the stimulation also helps to determine the nature of the movement. The assumption of special centres of coördination is superfluous. One other fact is of importance in experiments in extirpating and severing nervous connections, namely, that the division may bring about in those parts which are protoplasmically connected with the place of operation a change which is sometimes transitory, sometimes permanent—the so-called shock-effects. The highest degree of these shock-effects is attained in case of degeneration. It is a remarkable fact that, in an operation on the central nervous system, the effect of the shock is much greater in the part posterior to the place of operation than in the anterior part, toward the head. This may indicate that there is a constant current of impulses or influences in the direction from the brain to the posterior parts of the central nervous system. The interruption of these influences may be responsible for the condition which we call shock-effects and which may be transitory. These shock-effects are incomparably less strong in cold-blooded than in warm-blooded animals. We do not possess enough facts to enable us to give an explanation of the shock-effects.

BIBLIOGRAPHY.

1. HYDE, IDA H. *The Nervous Mechanism of the Respiratory Movements of Limulus Polyphemus. Journal of Morphology*, vol. ix., 1894.

2. LANGENDORFF, O. *Studien über die Innervation der Athembewegungen.* I. Mittheilung. *Archiv f. Physiologie*, 1880.

3. PORTER, W. T. *The Path of the Respiratory Impulse from the Bulb to the Phrenic Nuclei. Journal of Physiology*, vol. xvii., 1894–95.

4. VULPIAN. *Leçons sur la Physiologie générale et comparée du Système Nerveux.* Paris, 1866.

5. BETHE, A. *Vergleichende Untersuchungen über die Functionen des Centralnervensystems der Arthropoden. Pflüger's Archiv*, Bd. lxviii., 1897.

6. BETHE, A. *Das Centralnervensystem von Carcinus mænas. Archiv f. microskop. Anatomie und Entwicklungsgeschichte*, Bd. l., 1897 ; Bd. li., 1898.

7. STEINER, J. *Die Functionen des Centralnervensystems und ihre Phylogenese.* III. Abtheilung. *Die wirbellosen Thiere.* Braunschweig, 1898.

CHAPTER VIII

EXPERIMENTS ON MOLLUSKS

The literature on the functions of the central nervous system of Mollusks is extremely meagre. It is nevertheless valuable, as it furnishes us with further proofs of the theory that the simple and rhythmical spontaneity, as well as reflex processes, do not depend upon the brain or specific peculiarities of the ganglia. A Gastropod whose brain (*g*, Fig. 33)

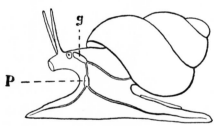

has been removed continues to move spontaneously. Steiner has observed this in a transparent pelagic species of snail, Pterotrachea, that is about 10 cm. long (1). The foot of this snail has been transformed into a swimming organ. Neither one- nor two-sided destruction of the supraœsophageal ganglion has the slightest influence upon the character and the

FIG. 33. SCHEMATIC REPRESENTATION OF THE CENTRAL NERVOUS SYSTEM OF A SNAIL (PALUDINA VIVIPARA).

g, brain; *P*, pedal ganglion. (Modified after Leydig.)

quantity of the spontaneous progressive movements. Destruction of the pedal ganglion, on the other hand, puts an end to all locomotion. Steiner concludes, therefore, that "the pedal ganglion alone has control of the entire locomotion of the animal." This anthropomorphic conclusion goes too far. The only conclusion we are justified in drawing from this observation is, that the protoplasmic connecting fibres between the skin and the foot-muscle of the animal pass through the gan-

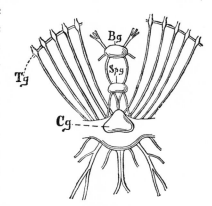

FIG. 34. BRAIN OF SEPIA.

Cg, cerebral ganglion; *Spg*, supraœsophageal ganglion; *Bg*, buccal ganglion; *Tg*, ganglia of the tentacles. (After Claus.)

glion. Steiner further attempted to see if he could produce circus-motions by means of a one-sided division of the œsophageal commissure in other Mollusks, Pleurobranchia and Aplysia. He succeeded no better than in Pterotrachea. One-sided destruction of the pedal ganglion in Cymbulia, however, caused paralysis of one-half of the locomotor organ. The animal naturally moved in a circle, for only one wing served as an oar.

The Cephalopods have an extremely complicated brain (Fig. 34). It consists of a dorsal and a ventral mass, each of which is composed of several ganglia.

o

The dorsal and ventral ganglia are connected by commissures. In addition, they possess a series of peripheral ganglia, the tentacle-ganglia (*Tg*, Fig. 34), for instance. It is of significance for the segmental theory that the tentacle-ganglia suffice to produce tentacle-reflexes, as v. Uexküll has shown in Eledone (2). It has been inferred from experiments on Vertebrates that peripheral ganglia cannot transmit reflexes.

Now, as regards experiments on the brain of Cephalopods, Steiner reports as follows concerning *Octopus vulgaris:* "If the dorsal ganglion on one side be removed, or both commissures of one side be severed, not the slightest change is visible in the life-processes of the animal, for it moves spontaneously as before, attacks its prey (*Carcinus mænas*) cleverly, and devours it. But the picture changes if the dorsal ganglion be entirely removed. To be sure the two forms of locomotion are preserved, for the animal creeps with the aid of its arms, or shoots like an arrow through the waves, when water is forced out of the mantle-cavity rhythmically. These movements are, however, no longer *spontaneous*, for they occur only when the animal is stimulated, neither does it take its food spontaneously. The normal octopus, which is endowed with *marked intelligence* [?], is wont to observe its surroundings most attentively, but now it sits indifferent to its surroundings, as though idiotic, and only its regular breathing gives evidence that it still lives. Vision is unimpaired, for it draws back when a stick is brought toward its eye." V. Uexküll's article on Eledone is more exhaustive than Steiner's. One of his observations, describing the extraordinarily excited condition of an animal whose cerebral ganglion had been removed, is worthy of mention. " All the reflexes seemed increased. When anyone approached the basin the Eledone that had undergone this operation swam off, while the normal animals remained quiet. There was an incessant play of colors. During the second night, in spite of the protecting net, it escaped and died on the floor of the laboratory." V. Uexküll concludes from this that there are inhibitory centres in the cerebral ganglion. We have seen that Bethe arrived at a similar conclusion in regard to the supraœsophageal ganglion of the Arthropods. We have discussed this possibility in connection with Maxwell's experiments on Nereis.

The arm-nerves originate in the pedal ganglion. But the latter is connected with the supraœsophageal ganglion directly by means of the anterior commissures and indirectly by means of the posterior commissures. Now it is of interest to know that the influence which the anterior part of the supraœsophageal ganglion exerts on the arm-movements when stimulated is exactly the opposite of that exerted by the posterior part; if the entire supraœsophageal mass between both pairs of commissures be separated by a frontal incision and both stumps be stimulated down deep, where the central ganglia are located, according to v. Uexküll, we obtain the following results : Stimulation of the anterior stump causes the cup-like suckers to take hold strongly ; stimulation of the posterior stump causes the suckers to let go and the arms to be withdrawn. Thus the antagonistic activities of the arms depend upon two different parts of the central nervous system. "An animal whose supraœsophageal mass has been divided in the vicinity of the first central ganglion behaves like an animal that is only able to take hold of objects. It grasps every object firmly and liberates itself again only with difficulty. It usually retains its hold and sits with extended arms, or crawls forward with the greatest difficulty. Such an animal placed on the back of a torpedo seizes it firmly with the arms, and no shocks of the electric organs are of avail to rid the fish of its burdensome rider. On the other hand, it is evident that the Eledone only participates in the ride involuntarily from the fact that it becomes dark brown and throws ink. If a normal Octopus by mistake grasps after a torpedo, it never remains in so dangerous a neighborhood more than a few seconds [I have observed this in Octopus, never in Eledone]." It seems to me that the conclusion to be drawn from these facts is, that the anterior and posterior parts of the supraœsophageal ganglion are connected with antagonistic muscle-groups. This relation is of interest in view of galvanotropic experiments, which we shall discuss later on. It is furthermore probable from v. Uexküll's experiments that the act of eating depends upon the integrity of the first central ganglion, while the second and third central ganglia are necessary for all the remaining functions of the arms, for instance, loco-motion and steering.

The fact discovered by v. Uexküll that the basal ganglion, when no longer connected with the central nervous system, produces coördinated chewing move-ments when stimulated is of great importance for the segmental theory. The skin and muscles are in this case connected by nerve-fibres which do not pass through the central nervous system but through a peripheral ganglion that v. Uexküll terms the bucco-intestinal ganglion. This is another fact that speaks for the idea that the ganglia are only to be considered as organs of transmission, that is, as connecting pro-toplasmic threads for reflexes, and not as bearers of mysterious reflex mechanisms.

BIBLIOGRAPHY.

1. STEINER, J. *Die Functionen des Centralnervensystems der wirbellosen Thiere.* *Sitzungsberichte der Berliner Academie der Wissenschaften*, 1890, i., p. 32.

2. V. UEXKÜLL. *Physiologische Untersuchungen an Eledone moschata.* *Zeitsch. f. Biologie*, Bd. xxxi., 1895.

3. STEINER, J. *Die Functionen des Centralnervensystems und ihre Phylogenese.* III. Abtheilung. *Die wirbellosen Thiere*, Braun-schweig, 1898.

CHAPTER IX

THE SEGMENTAL THEORY IN VERTEBRATES

1. The segmental arrangement of the central nervous system of Vertebrates is suggested by the arrangement of the spinal nerves. The number of segmental ganglia present in the head exceeds the number of cranial nerves. The auditory nerve and the vagus, for instance, originate from more than one segment each. Dohrn, Locy, and others have shown this. Locy states that there are originally fourteen segments in the head of the embryo of the shark, while there are only twelve cranial nerves. Physiology is more interested in the decision of this question than morphology, because upon it depends the theory of coördinated movements. The question of segmentation may also be of importance indirectly in connection with the idea of localisation in the cerebral hemispheres, for the so-called centres of the cerebral cortex are merely the places where the fibres from single segments of the central nervous system enter.

The spinal nerves originate in the spinal cord, and,

as has been said above, suggest externally its segmental character. Each has a ventral motor and a dorsal sensory root, and we desire to call attention to the fact that the dorsal root passes through a ganglion (the spinal ganglion). If the ventral root be severed, paralysis of the muscles of the corresponding segment occurs. If the dorsal root be severed, the corresponding segment becomes insensible, or, more properly speaking, the transmission of impulses which proceed from the periphery to the muscles of this segment and to the remaining segments becomes impossible. The operation itself, however, has still another influence on the tension of the muscles of the same segment (perhaps also of other segments). The amount of the muscle-tension under normal conditions varies (probably with the chemical conditions of the muscles). If a muscle be stretched with a certain weight it attains a certain length. But if the posterior nerve-roots be severed while the muscle is still nervously connected with its segment the muscle lengthens (E. v. Cyon). The operation causes a shock, in other words, probably a chemical change in the muscle. The nature of this change is as yet unknown. This influence of the posterior roots on the muscles shows itself also in the movements of an animal in which the posterior roots of the hind-legs have been severed : the movements of the legs are disturbed. It is known that the nerves of the brain are also of segmental origin, only in this case the inequalities of growth obliterate externally the segmental relations. From the fact that the chiefly sensory trigeminus, which may be considered as the posterior root of the facialis, possesses a peripheral ganglion (ganglion Gasseri), while the chiefly motor facialis has no peripheral ganglion, Bell concluded that the posterior roots of the spinal cord, which possess peripheral ganglia, are sensory, while the anterior roots, which possess no ganglia, are motor. Bell found (by means of vivisection) that division of the trigeminus produces disturbances in eating in those animals that take their food with the lips : these disturbances are caused, naturally, by the weakness of the corresponding muscles.

We will add a word here concerning the importance of the ganglion-cells for the preservation of the axis cylinder. The axis cylinder may be regarded as a protoplasmic extension of a ganglion-cell, which lives only as long as it is connected with the cell. Now the ganglion-cells of the dorsal roots are located in the spinal ganglion, those of the ventral roots in the ventral horns of the spinal cord. If the posterior roots be severed, that part of the fibres which is connected with the spinal cord degenerates, while the part that is connected with the spinal ganglion is preserved, and grows or regenerates. If the ventral roots be severed the peripheral stump degenerates, while the stump that is still connected with the spinal cord is preserved and grows. We may mention here briefly that the nerve-fibres of the posterior roots, according to Golgi's school, are not fused with the ganglion-cells of the posterior horns in the spinal cord, but are only in contact with them.[1] For the transmission of the impulse this fact is of no importance; it is not necessary in either case that the ganglion-cells of the posterior horn and the sensory nerves be grown together, they need only to be in sufficiently close contact. Engelmann called attention to these relations long ago in his excellent article on conduction in the ureter.

2. Sufficient data exist for proving the segmental localisation of reflexes in the spinal cord. In a dog whose spinal cord has been severed somewhere in the thoracic region the posterior part is entirely separated from the anterior part as far as the motor and sensory functions are concerned. Immediately after the operation severe shock-effects appear, but these are only temporary, and we shall return to this subject later. The interruption of the continuity is permanent, for in the central nervous system of higher animals no regeneration has been observed, but only a healing together of the cut surfaces by means of connective tissue. In such an animal the part located behind the point of division shows all the reactions which are possible in the corresponding segments. Goltz has proved this for dogs. Rubbing of the skin produces scratching movements of the hind-legs; erection of the penis and urination can be produced by stimulating the foreskin. The reflexes of the rectum and bladder and the vasomotor reactions are intact. We

---

[1] Apathy's publications arouse suspicion as regards the results obtained by Golgi's methods.

have already called attention to the fact that the respiratory movements are segmental processes. Goltz has shown that those reflexes in which the muscles of the arms are active are also segmental (2). During the period of heat the male frog clasps the female with his fore-limbs. If the head and back part of the body of a male frog be amputated during this time, so that only a piece consisting of the arms and the segmental piece of the spinal cord belonging with the arms remains, rubbing the skin on the ventral side of this piece suffices to produce the clasping reflex.

3. In considering the brain of Vertebrates we are obliged to deal with the brain of the cold-blooded animals, for the simple reason that in warm-blooded animals we cannot well perform brain-operations in the vicinity of the medulla oblongata without having the respiration cease. In cold-blooded animals the shock-effects are not so great. We have selected the brain of the frog as a type because it has been worked out the most carefully. It consists chiefly of the cerebral hemispheres (*GH*, Fig. 35), thalamus opticus (*Th.*, *O*), optic lobe, cerebellum (*KH*), and medulla oblongata. The diagram (Fig. 35) gives the origin of the nerves of the brain (V–XI). It is our aim to show in this chapter that the individual activities of the frog are dependent upon the segmental ganglia and that we have no right to speak of " centres " for the single activities unless the word centre is synonymous with the expression segmental ganglion.

We will first consider the coördinated progressive

movements. It was for a long time a dogma that progressive locomotive movements could only be performed by frogs that were still in possession of their cerebral hemispheres. This statement was made by Flourens. He observed that frogs devoid of the cerebral hemispheres no longer move spontaneously (3). Later on Schrader showed that this observation was not correct; that this lack of spontaneity only occurs when the thalami optici are injured (4). Are we to conclude from this that the power of spontaneous locomotion is located in the thalami

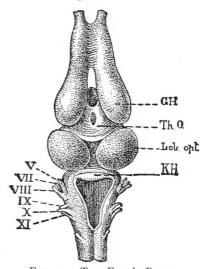

FIG. 35. THE FROG'S BRAIN.

GH, cerebral hemispheres; *Th.O*, thalamus opticus; *Lob. opt*, lobi optici; *KH*, cerebellum; *V–XI*, origin of the 5th to 11th brain-nerves. (After Wiedersheim.)

optici ? This would be wrong, for if the whole brain of a frog including the pars commissuralis of the medulla oblongata be removed, it seems " possessed of an irresistible desire to move ; it creeps about untiringly in an entirely coördinated manner and does not rest until it comes to a corner of the enclosure " (Schrader). It behaves like the Nereis in Maxwell's experiments which was deprived of its brain. Flourens made his localisation too high up. We wish to emphasise the fact that the frogs from which Schrader removed the whole brain, including the pars commissuralis, not only moved but were still able to climb. The condition of rest which appears after injury to the thalamus is thus not due to the loss of spontaneity. Steiner has also attempted to localise locomotion in a " centre." He found that frogs after losing the pars commissuralis of the medulla made no more progressive movements, and concluded from this that the sole and undivided control over all locomotions of the body belongs to this part (5 and 6). Schrader's contradictory results overthrow Steiner's conclusions. The latter author evidently made his observations on moribund animals, for his frogs survived the operation only a week at the most, while Schrader's lived many months and entirely recovered from the operation.

According to the segmental theory, on the other hand, it is to be expected that only those parts of the central nervous system are necessary for locomotion, which correspond to the segments of the muscles of the arms and legs. Thus it must be possible to obtain coördinated locomotion as long as the segmental ganglia of the muscles of the arms and legs are intact. This agrees with the result obtained by Schrader that after extirpating the whole brain, including the pars commissuralis, coördinated locomotion still occurs. We can go still farther and extirpate the whole medulla as far as the tip of the calamus scriptorius and still obtain coördinated locomotion. " Disturbance of the coördination in movements first begins with the apparent decrease in the ability to use the fore-legs, which becomes more and more apparent the nearer the incision approaches the origin of the brachial plexus from the tip of the calamus scriptorius. When this is reached the animal falls flat on its belly ; the fore-legs are no longer able to carry the body. If the animal be stimulated in the middle-line, for instance at the anus, the hind-legs throw the body forward. The forward extremities participate still with ' alternating ' but insufficient and peculiar trembling movements. A really coördinated progressive movement no longer takes place." We see again in this case the entire validity of the segmental theory : injuries of the spinal cord in the vicinity of the brachial plexus interfere with the walking movements only in so far as the coöperation of the fore-legs comes into consideration. The hind-legs, on the other hand, continue to function normally. Similar phenomena may be observed in fishes. They also cease to move about when the brain is removed up as far as the medulla oblongata. It would be quite wrong, however, to conclude from this that the centre of locomotion is located in the medulla oblongata. If the head of a shark be amputated the body swims about spontaneously. This experiment was made by Steiner. From the standpoint of the segmental theory this result was to be expected. The tail is the organ of locomotion for the shark, and only the corresponding segmental ganglia of the spinal cord are required for its activity. If the spinal cord of a young salamander be severed the swimming movements of the anterior and posterior parts are so well coördinated that it hardly seems credible that an operation has been performed. The same is true of the eel (8). The conditions are about the same as in the earthworm.

Rubbing the back of the frog causes it to croak, and in a frog whose brain has been removed as far as the medulla oblongata, this sound, as Goltz has found, can be produced with machine-like regularity (2). Viewed from the segmental standpoint this reflex is naturally conditioned by the integrity of the medulla, since it is there that the motor nerves for the production of the voice originate. The centre-theory had found a supposed " centre " for this reflex higher up in the brain.

4. The instinct for food and self-preservation was, like all the instincts, located in the cerebral hemispheres. An analysis of this instinct shows that it is composed of several reflexes, which are discharged successively. The first is a visual reflex; the frog catches only objects (flies, for instance) that are in motion. The opticus ends in the thalamus opticus, hence it is to be expected that the loss of the cerebral hemispheres would not prevent the frog from catching flies. Schrader found this to be the case. If previous authors believed their experiments to prove that the cerebral hemispheres are necessary for seeing, they were misled by the shock-effects of the operation, and in this way made the localisation too

high. Goltz had already shown, moreover, that the frog deprived of its cerebral hemispheres avoids obstacles. The same holds good for the fish that has lost the cerebral hemispheres. The first act in taking food thus consists in an optical reflex. As soon as the food comes in contact with the palate it arouses swallowing reflexes. These reflexes are completed by means of the vagus group. According to the segmental theory these reflexes should still be possible even when all the parts of the brain lying in front of the nuclei of the vagus have been removed. Such is the case. As long as the medulla oblongata is preserved the frog swallows the food that is put into its mouth.

The respiration of frogs is chiefly mouth- and neck-respiration. The corresponding nervous segments for these parts of the body lie in the medulla oblongata and in the beginning of the spinal cord. If the latter be severed behind the nœud vital (calamus scriptorius), as Schrader found, all the muscles whose nerves originate behind the place of division continue to participate in the respiration coördinately.

It was formerly assumed that the compensatory movements of frogs were dependent on organs of the mid-brain. Schrader found, however, that frogs whose brain had been extirpated as far as the medulla oblongata (the origin of the acusticus) still showed compensatory movements. The earlier physiologists were deceived by accidental effects of the operation. For the sake of completeness it should be mentioned, further, that the reflexes of wiping and warding off objects from the body of the frog are of a purely segmental character.

We have now given a review of the principal reactions of the frog and have found that no localisation of functions exists either in the brain or the spinal cord, that these are only segmental reflexes, just as in the Annelids and Arthropods. This conception was natural after results obtained from experiments on lower animals. That Schrader had foreseen it before the experiments reported here were known is proved by the closing sentence of his article on the frog's brain : " The series of experiments we have given teaches us that the central nervous system of the frog can be divided into a series of sections, each of which is capable of performing an independent function. It brings the central nervous system of the frog into closer relation with the central nervous system of the lower forms, which consists of a series of distinct ganglia that are connected by commissures. It speaks against the absolute monarchy of a single central apparatus and against the existence of different kinds of centres, and invites us to seek for the centralisation in a many-sided coupling of relatively independent stations." The question might be raised as to whether the activities of the frog which we have considered include *all* the reactions of this animal. The more complicated instincts are for the most part nothing more than series of segmental reflexes. I am inclined to recommend using the word chain-reflexes, whereby the performance of one reflex acts at the same time as the stimulus for setting free a second reflex. The taking of food may serve as an illustration of such a chain-reflex. The optic reflex of the moving fly produces the snapping reflex; the contact of the mouth-epithelium with the fly produces the swallowing reflex. Each of these reflexes is purely segmental. By taking into account the act of transmission, complicated acts can thus be resolved into a few segmental reflexes. A second fact must be taken into consideration if we wish to trace back the reactions of a frog to segmental reflexes, namely, that the irritability of the organs of its body changes. In the chapter on instincts we shall find how chemical conditions, especially, affect the form of the irritability of the animal, and how all conditions which bring about chemical changes in the body (temperature, food, sexual products) also modify its irritability. We shall then understand why the frog burrows at the beginning of the cold weather in autumn and puts in an appearance again with the awakening of spring, or, strictly speaking, with the beginning of the warm weather. The segmental reflex in the frog is, however, determined also by the irritability of the peripheral organs and the arrangement of the muscles. The segmental ganglion acts, in the main, simply as the protoplasmic connection between the surface of the body and the muscles.

The experiments of Goltz and of Goltz together with Ewald on the spinal cord of dogs prove that this law of segmental reflexes is also correct for dogs.

However, in warm-blooded animals every operation in the vicinity of the medulla oblongata is accompanied by such severe shocks to the segmental respiratory ganglia that the experimental proof is still wanting for the ganglia of the medulla in higher Vertebrates. It has been attempted with electrical stimuli, but such experiments only show that some kind of proto-plasmic connection exists between the stimulated spot and the segmental ganglia of the active muscles. The fact, for instance, that the respiratory movements are affected by stimulation of the third ventricle only proves that there are fibres at that place which go to the segmental respiratory ganglia. The conclusion, however, cannot legitimately be drawn from this that respiratory ganglia or " respiratory centres" are located in the third ventricle. Two facts have combined to hinder the development of the segmental theory. First, comparative physiology of the brain and embry-ology have never been duly considered. Because the *brain* of Vertebrates only reveals its segmental char-acter in the earliest embryological condition, only a small number of physiologists have thus far seriously believed that the segmental character of the central nervous system would furnish the key for comprehend-ing its functions. The second fact is disregard of the shock-effects upon those parts of the central nervous system situated behind the seat of the operation. It is possible that certain impulses ·flow constantly from the cephalic to the lower parts of the central nervous system. The stopping of these influences causes a change in the conditions of the segmental ganglia behind the seat of the operation. This change is the shock-effect.

Finally, the most important difference between the segmental conception of the central nervous system and the centre-theory may be pointed out. According to the latter theory, the central nervous system consists of a series of centres for as many different "functions." Each "function" is determined by the structure of its "centre." According to the segmental theory, there are only indifferent segmental ganglia in the central nervous system, and the different reactions or reflexes are due to the different peripheral organs and the arrangement of muscles. The centre-theory must remain satisfied with the mere problem of localising the apparent "seat" of a "function" without being able to give the dynamics of the reactions of an animal, as the latter depend in reality upon the peripheral structures, and not on the structures of the ganglia. For this reason the segmental theory alone will be able to lead to a dynamical conception of the functions of the central nervous system.

This difference may be made more apparent by comparison of these functions with those of the retina. The optical perception of forms consists in the power of single elements to determine, according to their position on the retina, different space-sensations. One retinal element may aid in bringing about many different pictures. Viewed from the segmental standpoint, we imagine the rôle of the central nervous system to be similar to this: the various elements or ganglia take the place of the retinal elements in the perception of forms. The same elements or ganglia participate in many "functions." Every element shares in the result according to the location of the segment, and other general or special qualities. But if we attempt to make clear to ourselves how the retina should act according to the centre-theory, we find that every retinal element would have to serve for the perception of one image only, that we could see only as many different images as we have retinal elements (for instance, rods). We do the centre-theory no injustice in making this comparison: its consistent representatives really assume that each image of memory is deposited in a special cell, that the number of the cells of the brain determines the number of the images of memory which are possible.

I wish to call the attention of the reader to the fact that Dr. A. Meyer has arrived, independently, at similar conclusions concerning the segmental character of the central nervous system of Vertebrates as those set forth in this chapter (9).

BIBLIOGRAPHY.

1. GOLTZ. *Ueber die Functionen des Lendenmarks des Hundes. Pflüger's Archiv*, Bd. viii., 1874.
2. GOLTZ. *Beiträge zur Lehre von den Nervencentren des Frosches.* Berlin, 1868. Verlag von Hirschwald.

3. FLOURENS, P.   *Recherches expérimentales sur les Propriétés et les Fonctions du Système Nerveux*, etc.   2. édit.   Paris, 1842.

4. SCHRADER, MAX E. G.   *Zur Physiologie des Froschgehirns. Pflüger's Archiv*, Bd. xli., 1887.

5. STEINER, J.   *Die Functionen des Centralnervensystems und ihre Phylogenese*.   Erste Abtheilung : *Untersuchungen über die Physiologie des Froschhirns*.   Braunschweig, 1885.

6. STEINER, J.   *Die Functionen des Centralnervensystems und ihre Phylogenese*.   II. Abtheilung, *Die Fische*.   Braunschweig, 1888.

7. GOLTZ, FR., and EWALD, J. R.   *Der Hund mit verkürztem Rückenmark. Pflüger's Archiv*, Bd. lxiii.   Bonn, 1896.

8. BICKEL.   *Beiträge zur Rückenmarksphysiologie des Aales. Pflüger's Archiv*, Bd. lxviii.

9. MEYER, ADOLF.   *Critical Review of the Data and General Methods and Deductions of Modern Neurology.   Journal of Comparative Neurology*, vol. viii., 1898.

CHAPTER X

SEMIDECUSSATION OF FIBRES AND FORCED MOVEMENTS

It is apparent from the foregoing that in the central nervous system of Vertebrates only segmental ganglia and only segmental reflexes appear. Superior centres, a " centre of coördination " for instance, cannot exist. Irritability and conductivity suffice to produce coördination in Medusæ, in the heart, in the respiration of Limulus, and in the movements of the earthworm and the salamander. Schrader has rightly expressed it : the nature of the nervous connections alone determines the coöperation of different segments in a common activity. Some of these connections require special mention, for instance, those in which decussation and semidecussation of fibres appear. Possibly the most familiar example of semidecussation is found in the optic nerves. Here the fibres cross, so that while each eye has its own special nerve each tract contains fibres from both eyes. The fibres of the temporal half of the retinæ pass through the chiasma uncrossed (that is, remain on the same side of the head and brain), the fibres which come from the nasal side of the retinæ undergo a decussation, *i. e.*, they cross to the other side of the head and brain. The left optic tract contains fibres from the temporal side of the left eye, and from the nasal, or internal, side of the right eye. If the left tract be cut, the left sides of both retinæ become blind, and the patient recognises nothing more in the right half of the field of vision. This is a case of hemianopia.

A similar semidecussation also occurs in the motor nerves of the eye. For the time being we may consider the various muscles of each eye as a unit. In the lateral movements of our eyes the rectus externus of one eye and the rectus internus of the other co-operate. If we assume an inherited connection between the retinal elements and the movements of the eyes, the right externus and the left internus must be innervated by the left half of the brain. The nerve-fibres of the externi must thus be crossed, those of the interni not crossed. The semidecussation in this case naturally occurs in the brain, and not peripherally. The pathological expression of this motor semidecussation is the *déviation conjugée*, which is a motor affection, corresponding to the sensory affection, hemianopia. We can only expect to find these semidecussations where symmetrical organs always receive equal innervations, as in the case of our eyes. Our arms and legs can move independently of each other, but in lower Vertebrates the case is different. The symmetrical fins of the fish receive equal innervations. I have shown that associated changes of position of the eyes and fins can be produced by destruction of an ear or the acoustic nerve (1). If we destroy in a shark the left auditory nerve or the left side of the medulla, where the auditory nerve enters, the left eye of the animal looks down, the right up. This change of position of both eyes suggests that the relative tension between the muscles that raise the eyes has changed. In the left eye the tension of the lowering muscles predominates over that of their antagonists; in the right eye the reverse is the case. The fins, likewise, show associated changes of position. The left fin is raised dorsally, the right is bent ventrally. While it can be said that both eyes are rolled about the longitudinal axis of the animal toward the left, the fins are rolled about the same axis to the right. Although the pectoral fins show the associated changes of position most clearly, these changes also exist in all the remaining fins, only with the difference that the amount of the change of position decreases the farther the segment is removed from the point of operation. The influence of the operation must decrease as the distance of a ganglion increases. The resistance to the transmission of the change increases with the distance.

These observations enable us to draw a conclusion concerning the connection of the muscles with the right and left halves of the corresponding ganglia. We may assume that a permanent *decrease*, but not a permanent *increase* in the tension of the muscles can result from the destruction of one part of the brain.

It is thus the muscles directly or indirectly connected with the left side of the medulla oblongata (in the acoustic segment) which show a decrease in tension after the destruction of the left ear. Accordingly, the left side of the medulla is connected with the raising muscles of the left eye and the lowering muscles of the right eye, as well as with the lowering muscles of the left pectoral fin and the raising muscles of the right pectoral fin. If we start with the idea that all the muscles of an eye or a fin form a common whole, a kind of semidecussation is present. It is, however, not only the muscles of the fins that undergo such changes of tension, but probably also the muscles of the spinal column.

If the symmetrical muscles of the organs of locomotion possess different tension, the usual stimuli for locomotion must naturally lead to unsymmetrical instead of symmetrical movements. When the lowering muscles predominate in the right pectoral fin and the raising muscles in the left, the animal, when these fins are used, will come under the influence of a couple of forces which must produce a rolling movement around the longitudinal axis of its body toward the left. As long as the animal swims slowly, rolling motions do not occur, for they are compensated for. The friction of the fish in the water will suffice to destroy a slight rolling motion. But if the animal attempts to swim rapidly, *e. g.*, if it be excited, it begins to roll. These rolling motions are called *forced movements*, a poorly selected term. The same movements have also been noticed in dogs and rabbits after an operation on one side of the medulla.

If a fish whose progressive movements are determined by the sculling motions of the tail turns to the right, the tail moves with greater force toward the right than toward the left. This condition might be made permanent if it were possible to weaken the muscles on the left side of the spinal column. This occurs when the right side of the acoustic segment of the medulla is destroyed. The fish moves in a circle toward the right. We also obtain circus-motions toward the right if we destroy the ventral portion of the left optic lobe. Hence, fibres must pass from the ventral portion of the left optic lobe to the right acoustic segment of the medulla. After such an operation, an increase in the tension of the skeletal muscles occasionally shows itself, for the fish may lie permanently bent into a circle without being able to straighten itself out again.[1] Such a fish can no longer swim straight ahead. The difference in the tension of the muscles on the two sides of the animal is, however, usually not so great, in which case the circus-motions will appear only spasmodically, for example, when the animal is excited.

One-sided division of the spinal cord and of the medulla behind the acoustic segment produces no forced movements (2 and 3). On the other hand, roll-

---

[1] If such a fish be decapitated the curvature of the body remains. It may even remain after death. We have to deal with an *organic* change in the muscles, caused by the operation.

ing and circus-motions may occur after injury to the brain in front of this segment, wherever places are met with which are directly or indirectly connected with the acoustic segment. This is the case, for instance, after a one-sided lesion of the pons or the cerebral hemispheres in rabbits and dogs. In both animals circus-motions occur after destruction of the cerebral hemispheres, in rabbits toward the intact side, in dogs toward the injured side. All the facts prove that the semidecussations take place in the vicinity of the acoustic segment and not farther down. In man, so far as I know, circus-motions have never been observed; this is probably due to his upright walk. It would be interesting to make the experiment of having patients afflicted with certain diseases (for instance, diseases of the inner ear) walk on all fours (with closed eyes) and to observe whether circus-motions occur.

As we have already mentioned, it is a well-known fact that in Arthropods after destruction of one half of the supraœsophageal ganglion circus-motions *can* occur. That they need not occur has been shown by Miss Hyde and also by Bethe (4 and 5). According to the investigations of the latter author these circus-motions in Invertebrates are called forth by very different disturbances in the muscle-tension. It is often due simply to a disturbance in the muscle-tension of the extremities of one side, the other side being apparently normal. In Crustaceans, associated changes of position of the extremities can also occasionally occur after destruction of one half of the supraœsophageal ganglion. In Cephalopods von Uexküll has

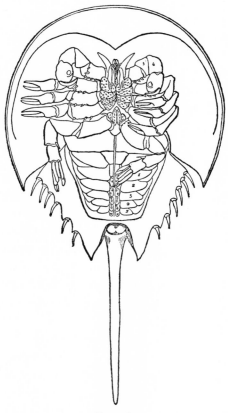

FIG. 36.

observed forced movements after lesion of an ear. Fig. 36 shows the predominance of the flexors of the legs over the extensors on the left side of the body of a Limulus. In this animal the right half of the brain had been destroyed and it showed circus-motions toward the left.

Steiner has made a peculiar application of the facts of forced movements. He imagines that the ability to move forward is a specific "function" of the brain, and has believed that it would be possible by means of this criterion to decide whether or not a ganglion of a lower animal should be called a brain. The

facts of comparative physiology do not favour this conception. Spontaneous progressive movements exist
in Infusoria which possess no nervous system, and even
in plant organisms, for example, in the swarmspores
of algæ. It is an important principle of physiological
epistemology that a phenomenon which occurs generally, cannot possibly be the *specific* function of an
organ which is peculiar to a few forms only. Steiner
soon found a fact that showed the erroneousness of
his theory, the fact that the decapitated shark continues to swim about in the tank. Schrader had likewise found that the frog without a brain is still able to
perform spontaneous progressive movements. Steiner
maintains further that "the brain is defined by the
general centre of movement in connection with the
action of at least one of the higher sensory nerves."
"In addition to its great simplicity this definition has
still another advantage, namely, that it is satisfied by a
single experiment; because of the two elements of
which the definition is made up, one element is always
given anatomically. This is the higher sensory nerve,
whose presence also vouches for its function. The
one experiment that it is necessary to make has to
prove that in addition to the sensory apparatus the general centre of movement also exists. The proof is then
complete if the one-sided removal of the central nervous part so changes the direction of the movements
of the animals that a circus-motion, which is generally
known by the name forced movement, takes the place
of a forward movement" (Steiner). This idea is

likewise erroneous and easily leads to absurdity. One-sided destruction of the cerebral hemispheres in man produces no forced movements. Thus, according to Steiner, the cerebral hemispheres should not belong to the brain. Second, according to Steiner, the ear must be a brain. One-sided lesion of the ear is sure to produce forced movements in a series of animals, and, moreover, the auditory nerve is a higher sensory nerve. I have mentioned this subject at this place because it is a typical illustration of what plays on words in physiology lead to. It is not our task to find a definition for the word *brain*, but to gain an insight into the functions of the central nervous system. It is of minor importance what name we give to the different parts of the central nervous system.

In connection with this chapter we wish to call attention to the more recent experiments of Sherrington and H. E. Hering, from which it seems to follow that with the innervation of a muscle the relaxation of its antagonist results simultaneously.

BIBLIOGRAPHY.

1. LOEB, J. *Ueber Geotropismus bei Thieren. Pflüger's Archiv*, Bd. xlix., 1891.

2. LOEB, J. *Ueber den Antheil des Hörnerven an den nach Gehirnverletzung auftretenden Zwangsbewegungen, Zwangslagen und associirten Stellungsänderungen der Bulbi und Extremitäten. Pflüger's Archiv*, Bd. l., 1891.

3. STEINER. *Die Functionen des Centralnervensystems und ihre Phylogenese.* II. Die Fische. Braunschweig, 1888.

4. BETHE, A. *Vergleichende Untersuchungen über die Functionen des Centralnervensystems der Arthropoden. Pflüger's Archiv,* Bd. lxviii., 1897.

5. BETHE, A. *Das Centralnervensystem von Carcinus mænas.* II. Mittheil. *Arch. f. mikroskop. Anatomie,* Bd. l., 1897.

6. STEINER, J. *Die Functionen des Centralnervensystems wirbelloser Thiere. Sitzungsberichte der Berliner Akademie der Wissenschaften.* 1890, I. S., 39.

CHAPTER XI

RELATIONS BETWEEN THE ORIENTATION AND FUNCTION OF CERTAIN ELEMENTS OF THE SEGMENTAL GANGLIA

The results of some investigations carried on by Garrey and myself showed that if a constant current be sent through a trough in which are larvæ of Amblystoma, peculiar changes may be observed in the postures of the animals (1). If the current passes through them longitudinally from head to tail (Fig. 37) the back becomes convex and the ventral side

FIG. 37. ATTITUDE OF AN AMBLYSTOMA UNDER THE INFLUENCE OF A GALVANIC CURRENT PASSING FROM HEAD TO TAIL.

FIG. 38. ATTITUDE OF AN AMBLYSTOMA WHEN THE GALVANIC CURRENT PASSES FROM TAIL TO HEAD.

concave. This change of position is occasioned by the muscles of the ventral side (the flexors of the spinal column) becoming more tense than the dorsal muscles (the extensors of the spinal column) from the passage of the current. On the other hand, if the current goes through the animal in the direction from tail to head both head (Fig. 38), and tail are raised. The body becomes more concave on the dorsal side and convex on the ventral side. The extensors of the spinal column become more tense than the ventral muscles. A pronounced opisthotonus exists. In order to show the phenomenon clearly the animal must be brought into the current gradually. If we continue to raise the intensity of the current, changes of position also take place in the legs. The changes in the hind-legs are more easily described than those in the fore-legs. If the current passes from head to tail the hind-legs are braced backward (Fig. 37), making the forward movement (to the anode) easier. If the current passes from tail to head the hind-legs are braced forward (Fig. 38), making the backward movement (to the anode) easier. How can these phenomena be explained? The current has two kinds of effects. A conduction of the current takes place through ions. Wherever the progress of ions is blocked in the central nervous system, an increase in their concentration will occur and this must be followed by physical or chemical alterations of the colloids. The progress of ions may be blocked by semipermeable membranes at the external limit of neurons or somewhere inside the neurons. Wherever anions are blocked different effects (anelectrotonus) will be produced than at places where the progress of kations is

11

blocked (katelectrotonus). The action of the various ions on nerve-elements is as yet unknown. The other effect of the current may consist in the migration of certain colloids in one direction and of water in the other direction.

If in the larvæ of Amblystoma the tension of the flexors of the spinal column predominates in a descending current (from head to tail) and the tension of the extensors of the spinal column predominates in an ascending current, this proves that *the nervous elements of the flexors and extensors in the central nervous system, which are affected by the ions, possess an opposite orientation.* Maxwell and I have developed more definite ideas concerning the orientation of these elements, but such details are for the time being of minor importance. I only wish to state that the relative orientation of these elements must be the same in every segment of the spinal cord; for when the spinal cord in the larvæ of Amblystoma is severed or the whole animal cut into several pieces the effects of the current remain the same. Since the article mentioned above was published I have found that crayfish (young and small specimens were used for these experiments) behave toward the current like Amblystoma larvæ. If the median-plane of the crayfish is in the direction of the lines of the current (which are all straight and parallel in these experiments) and the head is turned toward the anode, the flexors of the body contract. and the crayfish rolls itself into a complete ring, provided that the density of

the current is exactly right. The back is convex, the
ventral side concave. But if the current passes from
tail to head, the back becomes entirely straight, the
extensors being contracted to the utmost limit.[1] The
dorsal side cannot become concave because the exo-
skeleton of the crayfish does not allow it. Thus in
the body of the crayfish the motor elements of the
extensors and flexors which are affected by the current must have the same orientation as in the body of
Vertebrates. This holds good not only for the flexors
and extensors of the body but generally, as we shall
at once see.

We have already mentioned the fact that a constant current passing through Amblystoma larvæ in
the longitudinal direction affects not only the tension
of the flexors and extensors of the body, but also
the muscles of the extremities. The tension too is
changed in such a way, as has been already intimated,
that it renders movement toward the anode easy,
movement toward the kathode difficult. If, for instance, the current passes through the animal from
head to tail the hind-legs are braced backward and
the position of the fore-legs is changed correspondingly, so that the progressive movement of the animal is made easy, the backward movement difficult. If, however, the current passes from tail to
head the hind-legs are braced forward and the position of the fore-legs is changed correspondingly ; the

[1] It is necessary that in this experiment the intensity of the current be
increased very slowly.

animal can go backwards easily, while forward movement is difficult. In fact it is apparent that if the animals attempt to move in any direction while the current is passing through them they go toward the anode.[1]

From this fact it follows that, for the nervous apparatus of the progressive movements of Amblystoma, a close relation must exist between the orientation of the determinative elements of the motor nerves and their function : in fact the nervous elements which cause the progressive movements must have with regard to the longitudinal direction of the animal an orientation which is opposite to the orientation of those elements which cause the backward movement. Garrey and I had called attention to the fact that the observations of Blasius and Schweitzer show that other Vertebrates, for instance, young eels, behave like Amblystoma. The same also holds good for the shrimp. This last assertion is based upon a series of experiments made by Maxwell and myself (2). These experiments were made chiefly on Palæmonetes. This Crustacean uses the third, fourth, and fifth pairs of legs for its locomotion. The third pair pulls in the forward movement and the fifth pair pushes. The fourth pair generally acts like the fifth and requires no further attention. If a current be sent through the animal longitudinally, from head to tail, and the strength increased gradually, a change soon takes place in the

[1] This explains the galvanotropic gatherings observed by Hermann, Blasius and Schweitzer, and others.

position of the legs. In the third pair the tension of the flexors predominates, in the fifth the tension of the extensors. The animal can thus move off easily with the pulling of the third and the pushing of the fifth pairs of legs, that is to say, the current changes the tension of the muscles in such a way that the forward movement is rendered easy, the backward difficult. Hence it can easily go toward the anode, but only with difficulty toward the kathode. If a current be sent through the animal in the opposite direction, namely, from tail to head, the third pair of legs is extended, the fifth pair bent; that is, the third pair can push and the fifth pair pull. The animal will thus go backward easily and forward with difficulty. We see here again that the nervous elements of the central nervous system which bring about the forward movements have the opposite orientation as regards the longitudinal axis of the animal from the nervous elements which bring about the backward movement. But we can go still further in the development of this law. Palæmonetes can not only walk, but is also a good swimmer, and it can swim backwards as well as forwards. In swimming forwards the swimming appendages, among which the tail fin must be counted, push backwards forcibly and forwards gently; in swimming backwards the opposite occurs. If the current be sent through Palæmonetes in the direction from head to tail[1] the swimming

---

[1] The tail fin behaves toward the current like the abdominal swimming appendages and not like the body. This must be taken into consideration in galvanotropic experiments.

appendages, and the tail also, are stretched backward or dorsad to their fullest extent. This proves that the tension of the muscles that move those organs backwards is greater than that of their antagonists. The shrimp can thus swim forwards toward the anode easily under the influence of such a current, but backwards only with difficulty. If the current passes through in the opposite direction (from tail to head), however, the tail and the ventral appendages are turned forward. The tension and the development of energy now predominate in those muscles which move the swimming appendages backwards. In this way the animal can swim backwards easily, while it is difficult or impossible for it to swim forwards. Hence the nervous elements, which determine the forward-swimming, must also have the same orientation in regard to the longitudinal axis of the animal as those elements which determine the walking forwards, while the nervous elements for swimming backwards have the opposite orientation.

The fact yet remains to be considered that Palæ-monetes, like many other Crustacea, can also move sideways. This movement is produced by the pulling of the legs on the side toward which the animal is moving (contraction of the flexors), while the legs of the other side push (contraction of the extensors). If a current be sent transversely, say from right to left, through the animal, the legs of the right side assume the flexor-position, those of the left side the extensor-position. In the legs of the right side the flexors produce more energy, in the legs of the left side the extensors. The transverse current assists the animal in moving to the right toward the anode and prevents it from moving to the left toward the kathode. Hence the nervous elements which produce the sidewise movement of the crayfish toward the right must have the opposite orientation in regard to the longitudinal axis from the nervous elements which produce the sidewise movement to the left.

Maxwell and I had attempted to give a picture of the arrangement of those elements on the assumption that they are the motor neurons. No reason exists, however, for regarding the ganglion-cell *in toto* as the point of action for the chemical effect of the ions set free. It may be any element inside of the ganglion-cells, or even of the fibre itself ; it is not even necessary that this element should be especially noticeable histologically. Life-phenomena are determined by physical and chemical conditions which are outside the realm of histology. But whatever it is, it is certain *that those determinative elements in the central nervous system whose activity produces movements of the body, have a fixed orientation in the body, which evidently stands in some simple relation to the direction of the movement which is produced by it.*

The idea of such a simple relation between the orientation of nervous elements and the direction of motion produced by them is no more strange than the facts observed in the stimulation of the horizontal canal of the labyrinth. If this canal be slightly touched motions of the eyes or head occur in the plane of this canal. In this case we have to deal with a simple relation between the orientation of the canal and the plane in which the organs or the whole body of the animal move. This fact is just as mysterious as the more general facts mentioned in this chapter. I am inclined to assume that the peculiar relation between the semicircular horizontal canal and the motions produced by the stimulation of this canal finds its explanation through the facts mentioned in this chapter. It is possible that the central endings of the nerve of the horizontal canal are connected with the motor elements in the medulla whose activity produces motions in the plane of the horizontal canal. When Flourens made his experiments on the semicircular canals he found that there was a striking resemblance between the effects of a destruction of the canals and the sectioning of the crura cerebelli. He came to the conclusion that there must be a simple relation between the direction of the fibres of the crura cerebelli and the motion produced by them (3). His observations are not in all points correct; yet with some modification his fundamental idea remains true. The next chapter, on the cerebellum, will give us some more data about his observations.

It is possible for us to conceive from this how it happens that the same optic stimulus or the same space-perception is able to direct our eyes toward a certain point, to turn our head in that direction, to guide our finger thither, or to bring our legs into such activity that our body arrives at that place. *It is possible that the elements of the central nervous system which become active in this way all have the same orientation in each segment, and what we call an innervation may be a process in which the orientation of the elements plays a rôle.* The effect of the electric current might be an example of such a process. This problem of the physiology of coördinated movement which we touch upon here has always seemed to me the most mysterious in the whole physiology of the central nervous system, and the way offered here of reaching a simple solution seems to me worthy of mention. The whole conception can easily be classified under the segmental conception of the central nervous system. Movements of the eyes, head, arms, and legs depend upon as many different segmental ganglia. Each of these ganglia has some features in common with every other ganglion, for instance the orientation and arrangement of the elements (neurons?). If a process of such a nature that it can only stimulate elements oriented in a certain way in each ganglion spreads through the segmental ganglia, it must produce a movement in exactly the same direction in the appendages of each segment. This does away with the necessity of imagining artificial connections of the neurons which would be able to produce such a series of coördinated motions in different limbs and segments.

If the question be raised, however, as to how it happens that a simple relation exists between the orientation of the motor nerve-elements and the movement or progressive movement produced by them, we must again refer to the simple segmental relations of the first embryonic formation that remains better preserved in the central nervous system than in the muscles. The problem with which we have to deal here is ultimately a problem of embryology.

BIBLIOGRAPHY.

1. LOEB, J., and WALTER E. GARREY. *Zur Theorie des Galvanotropismus.* II. Mittheilung. *Versuche an Wirbelthieren. Pflüger's Archiv,* Bd. lxv., 1896.

2. LOEB, J., and S. S. MAXWELL. *Zur Theorie des Galvanotropismus. Pflüger's Archiv,* Bd. lxiii., 1896.

3. FLOURENS, P. *Fonctions du Système nerveux.* Paris, 1842.

CHAPTER XII

EXPERIMENTS ON THE CEREBELLUM

The experiments on the cerebellum support to a certain extent the observations mentioned in the preceding chapter.

The cerebellum, like the cerebral hemispheres, is a structure which clearly expresses inequality of growth. Both may be considered as evaginations and appendages of the segmental nervous system. The cerebellum is connected with the central nervous system by three crura, the crura cerebelli ad medullam oblongatam, the crura cerebelli ad pontem, and the crura cerebelli ad corpora quadrigemina. The latter extend forward in a pretty straight line, the first extend backward, and the peduncles to the pons at right angles to both. Magendie discovered and Flourens confirmed the fact that lesion of these tracts possessing so characteristic an orientation to the chief axes of the body produces "forced" movements whose direction bears a simple relation to the orientation of the severed peduncle. If a peduncle of the pons be severed on one side the animal rolls about its longitudinal axis. If the crura cerebelli that extend forward be severed the animal rushes forward with great force ; if the crura cerebelli ad medullam oblongatam be severed the animal goes backwards or shows a tendency to turn somersaults backwards. " La direction des mouvements produits par la section des fibres de l'encéphale est donc toujours determinée par la direction de ces fibres" (Flourens).

Flourens called attention to the analogy of these phenomena with those he observed after lesion of the semicircular canals. This analogy, however, does not exist just as he states it. He compares the effect of the one-sided division of the pons with the division of a horizontal canal. This is not correct. So far as I know, such a lesion does not produce rolling motions about the longitudinal axis in any animal. On the other hand, destruction of a whole ear, probably in most cases, causes rolling motions. Flourens states further that after destruction of the anterior canals an animal turns somersaults forwards, after destruction of the posterior canals backwards. Flourens assumes that the nerves of the three canals continue into the corresponding peduncles of the cerebellum, and that this origin of the nerves is the cause of the phenomena that we observe after lesion of the single semicircular canals (3). But this is probably not correct, since the auditory nerve ends in the medulla. It is possible, however, that the cerebellum is connected with the same motor elements in the medulla with which the acoustic nerve is connected. The cerebellum might thus appear as an appendage of the acoustic segments.

This harmonises with the results Ferrier obtained from his stimulation experiments (1). He found that stimulation of the different parts of the cerebellum causes associated movements of the eyes, and that the direction of the movement changes with the position of the electrodes. The head also moves in the same direction as the eyes. Movements of the limbs were also observed, but it could not be determined whether or not they were associated with the movements of the head. From this we may conclude that possibly or probably the movements which are produced by stimulation of the cerebellum are somewhat related to those movements which are produced by stimulation or injury of the semicircular canals, only that the stimulation experiments on the cerebellum, according to Ferrier, often yield no results.

Extirpation of the cerebellum leaves the sensory and psychic functions of the animal undisturbed. It is only in the movements that peculiar disturbances appear, which are described differently by the different authors. The motions of the animals resemble somewhat those of a patient suffering from St. Vitus's dance, inasmuch as they do not reach the intended aim and are often excessive in character. It is necessary that the head of a dog whose cerebellum has been injured be held in the dish when it eats, for if not held every effort sends the head so much too far that the animal is not able to get its food. This disturbance is most pronounced immediately after the operation and may disappear more or less after a certain time.

Such disturbances also show themselves in the limbs. The animal often staggers about like an intoxicated person and finds difficulty in keeping itself on its legs. All these peculiarities perhaps point ultimately to a decrease in the tension of the skeletal muscles. The measured movements of the normal animal are only possible if the tension of the antagonistic muscles is so great that excessive movements cannot take place. But if the muscles of the spinal column are relaxed in the dog without the cerebellum, as has been maintained (and apparently with good reason), every intended movement can go wide of its aim.

According to the results of Luciani's numerous experiments, weakness or relaxation of the muscles seems to form the most constant factor in the effects of operations on the cerebellum. The affected groups of muscles, however, seem to vary with the position of the part of the cerebellum which is destroyed. Flourens, who attributed special functions to each section of the brain, maintained that the cerebellum was the general centre of coördination, because lesions of the cerebellum bring about the above-mentioned disturbances. Luciani (2) has shown, however, that some of the dogs that had lost the cerebellum were still able to perform coördinated swimming motions in the water and even coördinated walking motions. The weakness of all or of certain groups of muscles may lead to ataxic disturbances, but in some cases these may be very slight. Thus we see that Flourens's theory that the cerebellum is an organ of coördination is not correct. It may be too that a part of the disturbances observed after lesion of the cerebellum are due to secondary effects of the operation on the medulla or the corpora quadrigemina.

This latter conception is supported by comparative physiology. In fishes and frogs, in which the shock-effects are slight, the cerebellum can be removed without producing any disturbance in the behaviour of the animals (Vulpian, Steiner). In sharks, whose cerebellum is strongly developed, I myself have made numerous division-experiments and numerous experiments on partial or total extirpation of the cerebellum, and no change whatever took place in the behaviour of the animals. It is impossible and unjustifiable in this case to talk of a definite " function " of the cerebellum.

It may be well, in consideration of what has been said in the preceding chapter and of observations which will be discussed later on concerning the results of lesions of the cerebral hemispheres, to remind the reader of a hypothesis made by Magendie. He saw animals walk or fly backwards permanently after lesion of a certain part of the medulla oblongata. He saw further that a lesion of the corpora striata produces an impulse to run forwards. Finally he observed the rolling motions of the animals about their longitudinal axis after one-sided lesion of the pons. He makes the following remark in this connection : " Comme notre esprit a besoin de s'arrêter à certaines images je dirai qu'il existe dans le cerveau quatre impulsions spontanées ou quatre forces qui seraient placées aux extrémités de deux lignes, qui se couperaient à angle droit, l'une pousserait en avant, la deuxième en arrière, la troisième de droit à gauche en faisant rouler le corps, la quatrième de gauche à droite en faisant exécuter un mouvement semblable de rotation. Dans les diverses expériences d'où je tire ces conséquences les animaux deviennent des espèces d'automates montés pour exécuter tels ou tels mouvements et incapables d'en produire aucun autre." The last statement goes too far, but Magendie's main thought deserves more consideration than it has heretofore received from physiologists. The galvanotropic facts mentioned in Chapter XI. show most conclusively that in Crustaceans and Vertebrates there exists a relation between the orientation and function of certain motor elements, and a similar relation also finds expression in the experiments on the horizontal semicircular canal.[1]

[1] Dr. Lyon has shown that only the stimulation of the horizontal canal gives rise to motions in the plane of this canal, while the same result cannot be obtained with any degree of certainty through a stimulation of the two other canals (4).

BIBLIOGRAPHY.

1. FERRIER. *The Functions of the Brain.* New York, 1886.
2. LUCIANI, LUIGI. *Das Kleinhirn.* Leipzig, 1893.
3. FLOURENS, P. *Fonctions du Système nerveux.* Paris, 1842.
4. LYON, E. P. *A Contribution to the Comparative Physiology of Compensatory Motions. The American Journal of Physiology,* vol. iii., 1900.

CHAPTER XIII

ON THE THEORY OF ANIMAL INSTINCTS

1. The discrimination between reflex and instinctive actions is chiefly conventional. In both cases we have to deal with reactions to external stimuli or conditions. But while we speak of reflex actions when only a single organ or a group of organs react to an external stimulus, we generally speak of instincts when the animal as a whole reacts. In such cases the reactions of the animal, although unconscious, seem often to be directed towards a certain end. A fly acts instinctively when it lays its egg on objects which serve the hatching larvae as food. We call the periodical migrations of animals instinctive. We call it instinctive when certain animals conceal themselves in cracks and crevices where they are safe from persecution. But the purposeful character of instincts cannot be used to distinguish them from reflexes, as a great many of the reflexes are also purposeful, for instance, the closing of the eyelid if the conjunctiva be touched or the wiping off of acetic acid that is put on the skin of a decapitated frog. On the other hand, it cannot be said that every instinctive action is purpose-

ful, for instance, the flying of the moth into the flame.

In many cases the greater complication of instinctive actions compared with simple reflex actions is due to the fact that in the instinctive actions we have to deal with a chain of reflexes in which the first reflex becomes at the same time the cause which calls forth the second reflex. The taking up of food by the frog is a good illustration of this. The motion of the fly causes an optical reflex which results in the snapping motion. The contact of the fly with the mucous membrane of the pharynx sets free a second reflex, the swallowing reflex, which brings the fly into the œsophagus. If it be true that the instincts belong to the same class of processes as the reflexes, their relation to the central nervous system should be the same. We have seen that as far as reflexes are concerned, the nervous system only acts as a protoplasmic conductor between the periphery (sense organs) and the muscles. I think it is possible to show that this is also true for instincts. In order to prove this, we shall have to go into an analysis of the instincts. We shall select for our analysis such simple cases of instincts as depend upon tropisms.

2. We have seen that when certain Crustaceans, for instance Palæmonetes, are subjected to the effect of a galvanic current such changes of tension take place in the muscles of the appendages that movement toward the anode becomes easier, and toward the kathode more difficult. The result is that if the current is

continued long enough, all the animals collect at the positive pole. When this process is observed without a careful analysis, it seems as though these Crustaceans possessed the instinct to move toward the anode, just as the moths possess the instinct to move into the flame. The flight of the moth into the flame is in reality only the result of a tropism,—heliotropism, which differs from galvanotropism chiefly in that the rays of light take the place of the curves of the current. The reader knows that certain plants when exposed to the light on one side, for instance, when cultivated at a window, bend their tip toward the window until the tip of the stem is in the direction of the rays of light. The tip then continues to grow in the direction of the rays. We call this dependence of orientation on light heliotropism. We speak of positive heliotropism when the organ bends towards the source of light, of negative heliotropism when the organ bends away from it. It is generally assumed that the light has a chemical effect in these cases.

The relations of symmetry in plants and animals play an important part in these phenomena. We will take, by way of illustration, the stem of a hydroid, Eudendrium that is being raised near a window. I have found that it bends toward the window like a positively heliotropic plant under the same conditions. The process may be described as follows : The light strikes the Eudendrium-stem from the side. A contraction of the protoplasm on that side ensues and a greater resistance is thus offered to the increase in length on this side than on the opposite side. The result is that the stem bends and becomes concave on the side toward the light. As soon, however, as the bending has progressed so far that the stem comes into the direction of the rays of light, all the symmetrical elements are struck by the light at the same angle. The intensity of light is thus equal at symmetrical points, and there is no longer occasion for the stem to leave this direction. It thus continues to grow in the direction of the rays of light. Negatively heliotropic elements, roots, for instance, differ from positively heliotropic elements in that the light produces a relaxation of the protoplasm. Hence when the light comes from one side, the resistance to the growth on that side will be less than on the opposite side, and the tip will bend away from the source of light. As soon as the tip comes into the direction of the rays of light and the symmetrical points are all struck by them at the same angle, the intensity of the light on both sides is the same, and every cause for leaving this direction is removed. It has been known for a long time that many animals are " attracted " by the light and fly into the flame. This was considered a special instinct. It was said that these animals loved the light, that curiosity drove them into it. I have shown in a series of articles, the first of which appeared in January, 1888, that all these actions are only instances of those phenomena which were known in plants as heliotropism.

It was possible to show that the heliotropism of animals agreed in every point with that of plants. If a moth be struck by the light on one side, those muscles which turn the head toward the light become more active than those of the opposite side, and correspondingly the head of the animal is turned toward the source of light. As soon as the head of the animal has this orientation and the median-plane (or plane of symmetry) comes into the direction of the rays of light, the symmetrical points of the surface of the body are struck by the rays of light at the same angle. The intensity of light is the same on both sides, and there is no more reason why the animal should turn to the right or left, away from the direction of the rays of light. Thus it is led to the source of the light. Animals that move rapidly (like the moth) get into the flame before the heat of the flame has time to check them in their flight. Animals that move slowly are affected by the increasing heat as they approach the flame ; the high temperature checks their progressive movement and they walk or fly slowly about the flame. The more refractive rays are the most effective in animals just as in plants (1).

Hence the " instinct " that drives animals into the light is nothing more than the chemical—and indirectly the mechanical—effect of light, an effect similar to that which forces the stem of the plant at the window to bend toward the source of light, or which forces Palæmonetes to collect at the anode. The moth does not fly into the flame out of " curiosity," neither is it " attracted " by the light ; it is only *oriented* by it and in such a manner that its median-plane is brought into the direction of the rays and its head directed toward the source of light. In consequence of this orientation its progressive movements must lead it to the source of light.

We now come to the most important question in this chapter, namely, the relation of the central nervous system to the instincts. As long as such apparently complex things as the instincts are not analysed but treated as entities, it is easy to believe that they are based upon very mysterious nervous structures. It would harmonise with the centre-theory to assume for the moth a " flying-into-the-flame centre," [1] and to seek for its localisation in the central nervous system. The fact that the flying of the moth into the flame is nothing but positive heliotropism, and the fact that the positive heliotropism of animals is identical with the positive heliotropism of plants, proves that this reaction must depend upon conditions which are common to *animals and plants.* Plants, however, possess no central nervous system, therefore I believe that it is impossible for the heliotropic reactions of animals to depend upon *specific* structures of the central nervous system. It is much

[1] Steiner tries indeed to "explain" the righting motions of the starfish by the assumption of a " righting centre " in the central nervous system. He does not consider the possibility that contact stimuli and the irritable structures at the periphery may be sufficient for this reaction, and that the nerves act only as protoplasmic conductors between the skin and the muscles.

more probable that they are determined by properties which are common to animals and plants. From what has been said above it is easy to infer what these properties are : First, heliotropic animals as well as heliotropic plants must contain a substance on their surfaces which undergoes a chemical change when subjected to the influence of the light, and this change must be able to produce changes of tension in the contractile tissue. Second, heliotropic animals as well as heliotropic plants possess symmetry of form and a corresponding distribution of the irritabilities. These two groups of conditions determine the heliotropic reaction unequivocally. But what has the central nervous system to do with this " instinct " of the moth to fly into the flame, or, as we may now say, with its heliotropism ? I believe nothing more than that the nervous system contains a series of segmental ganglia which establish the protoplasmic connection between the skin and muscles. If we destroy the central nervous system, the heliotropic reactions in many animals cease, but mainly for the reason that the connection between the skin, or the eyes, which are affected by the light, and the muscles, is interrupted. Hence it would be just as wrong to assume a specific centre for the flight of the moth into the flame as it would to assume a specific centre for the going of Palæmonetes to the anode.

3. We will select another instinct, namely, the habit many animals have of crawling into cracks and crevices. This " instinct " is very prevalent in the

animal kingdom, especially among insects, worms, etc.
This is called an instinct of self-preservation, and it
is assumed that the animal thus escapes from its
pursuers. The centre theory would assume a special
centre for this instinct. This is, however, only another instance of a simple tropism. Many plants
and animals are forced to orient their bodies in a certain way toward solid bodies with which they come in
contact. I have given this kind of irritability the
name stereotropism. Like the positive and negative
heliotropism and geotropism, there is also a positive
and negative stereotropism, and there are also stereotropic curvatures. I have found, for instance, that
when a Tubularia is brought in contact with a solid
body, the polyp and the growing tip bend away from
the body while the stolon sticks to it. The polyp
is negatively stereotropic and the stolon positively
stereotropic. Stereotropism plays a very important
part in the processes of pairing and the formation of
organs. The tendency of many animals to creep
into cracks and crevices has nothing to do with self-
concealment, but only with the necessity of bringing
the body on every side in contact with solid bodies.
I have proved this, for instance, in a peculiar species
of butterfly, Amphipyra, that is a fast runner. As
soon as free, it runs about until it finds a corner or a
crack into which it can creep. I placed some of these
animals in a box, one half of which was covered with
a non-transparent body, the other half with glass. I
covered the bottom of the box with small glass

plates which rested on small blocks, and were raised
just enough from the bottom to allow an Amphipyra
to get under them.   Then the Amphipyra collected
under the little glass plates, where their bodies were
in contact with solid bodies on every side, not in the
dark corner where they would have been concealed
from their enemies.   They even did this when in so
doing they were exposed to direct sunlight.   This reaction also occurred when the whole box was dark.   It
was then impossible for anything but the stereotropic
stimuli to produce the reaction.   The same phenomenon may be observed in worms, for instance, in
Nereis.   If an equal number of Nereis and glass tubes
be placed in a dish of sea-water, we may be sure
that after a time we shall find a worm in each tube.
This even occurs when the tubes are exposed to the
direct rays of the sun, which kill the worms.   This is
also a reaction which is common to plants, hydroids,
and animals possessing a central nervous system,
which must therefore depend upon circumstances
which have nothing directly to do with the central
nervous system.   These circumstances are apparently
chemical effects in the skin, which are produced in
these forms by the contact with solid bodies.   This is
another instance where the central nervous system
only plays the part of a protoplasmic conductor.   It
would be entirely wrong to attempt to look for a
" centre of self-concealment " in these animals.   This
is confirmed by experiments on worms that have been
cut into pieces.

4. We will now turn our attention to the consideration of some more complicated instincts. It always seemed to me one of the most wonderful arrangements in nature that, in many species, the female lays her eggs in places where the newly born larvæ find just the kind of food they require. The fly lays its eggs on decaying meat, cheese, or similar material, and it is on these substances that the young larvæ feed. I have often placed pieces of lean meat and pieces of fat from the same animal side by side on the window-sill, but the fly never failed to lay its eggs on the meat and not on the fat. I further tried to raise the larvæ on fat. As was to be expected, they did not grow, but soon died. It was possible to discover the mechanics of the peculiar instincts of the mothers through experiments on the young larvæ. The larvæ are oriented by certain substances which radiate from a centre, and this orientation takes place in the same way as in the orientation of heliotropic animals by the light. The *centre of diffusion* takes the place of the *source* of light, and the *lines of diffusion* (that is the straight lines along which the molecules move from the centre of diffusion into the surrounding medium—*i. e.*, the air) the place of the rays of light. The chemical effects of the diffusing molecules on certain elements of the skin influence the tension of the muscles, as the rays of light influence the tension of the muscles in heliotropic animals. The orientation of an organism by diffusing molecules is termed chemotropism, and we speak of positive chemotropism

when the animal is forced to bring its axis of symmetry into the direction of the lines of diffusion and to turn its head toward the centre of diffusion. In such an orientation every pair of symmetrical points on the surface of the animal is met by the lines of diffusion at the same angle. It can easily be shown that larvæ of the fly are positively chemotropic toward certain chemical substances which are formed, for instance, in decaying meat and cheese, but which are not contained in fat. The substances in question are probably volatile nitrogenous compounds. The young larvæ are probably led by those substances to the centre of diffusion in the same way as the moth into the flame. The female fly possesses the same positive chemotropism for these substances as the larvæ, and is accordingly led to the meat. As soon as the fly is seated on the meat, chemical stimuli seem to throw into activity the muscles of the sexual organs, and the eggs are deposited on the meat. It may also be possible that at the time when the fly is ready to deposit its eggs the positive chemotropism is especially strongly developed. It is only certain that neither experience nor volition plays any part in these processes. If the question be raised as to what is necessary in order to produce these reactions, the answer is, first, the presence of a substance in the skin or certain parts of the skin (sense-organs) of the animal which is altered by the above-mentioned volatile substances contained in the decaying meat, and second, the bilateral symmetry of the body. The central nervous system plays no other rôle in this than that it forms the protoplasmic bridge for the conduction from the skin to the muscles. In organisms in which this conduction is possible without a central nervous system, in plants, for instance, we also find the same reactions.

5. We find another instance of a preservative instinct in the young caterpillars of many butterflies. The larvæ of *Porthesia chrysorrhœa* creep out of the eggs in the autumn and winter in colonies in a nest on trees or shrubs. The warm spring sun drives them out of the nest and they crawl up on the branches of the tree or shrub to the tip, where they find their first food. After having eaten the tips, they crawl about until they find new buds or leaves, which in the meantime have come out in great numbers. It is evident that the instinct of the caterpillars to crawl upwards, as soon as they awake from the winter sleep, saves their lives. Were they not guided by such an instinct, those that crawled downwards would die of starvation. What rôle does the central nervous system play in these instincts?

I have found that the young caterpillars of Porthesia are oriented by the light. Until they have taken food they are positively heliotropic. This positive heliotropism leads them to the tips of the branches where they find their food. During the winter they are stiff and do not move. The higher temperature of the spring brings about chemical changes in their bodies, and these chemical processes cause them to move. But the direction of their movements is determined by the light. Out-of-doors, where the diffused light strikes the animal on all sides, every ray of light can be resolved into a horizontal and a vertical component. The horizontal components destroy each other, and only the effect of the vertical components remains. Hence the animals are forced, as a result of their positive heliotropism, to crawl upwards until they reach the tip of a branch. They are held there by the light. The chemical stimuli which are transmitted to the animal by the young buds produce the eating movements. In this instinct, which is necessary for the preservation of life, we have another instance of simple positive heliotropism, and the central nervous system plays only the rôle of a protoplasmic connection between the skin and contractile tissue, which in plants is performed just as successfully by undifferentiated protoplasm.

We have seen, however, that these same caterpillars leave the tips of the branches as soon as they have eaten and crawl downward. Why does the light not hold them on the highest point permanently? My experiments showed that these caterpillars are only positively heliotropic as long as they remain unfed ; after having eaten they lose their positive heliotropism. This is not the only instance of this kind, for I have found a series of facts which show that chemical changes influence the irritability of the animal toward light. We can imagine that the taking up of food leads to the destruction of the substances in the skin of the animal which are sensitive to light, upon which substances the heliotropism depends, or that through the consumption of food the action of these substances is indirectly prevented.

6. The analysis of other instincts, for instance, the migratory instinct of animals, leads to the same result as the analysis of the protective instincts. These instincts are not functions of certain localised " centres," but of irritabilities of certain peripheral structures and of the connection of the same with the muscles, whereby the central nervous system only serves as a protoplasmic connection. It would naturally be more interesting to select for our discussion the migrations of birds, but it is difficult to make laboratory experiments on this subject, and without laboratory experiments we cannot easily obtain reliable results. For this reason I have made use of another class of periodic migrations, namely, the periodic depth-migrations of pelagic animals. A great number of these animals begin a vertical upward migration toward the surface of the ocean in the evening, while in the morning they migrate downwards. It is a remarkable fact that these forms never go below a depth of four hundred metres in their downward migrations. This fact suggests that the light is the controlling power in these depth-migrations. Water absorbs the light, and the thicker the layer of water the more the light is absorbed. It has been found that at a depth of four hundred metres a photographic plate is no longer affected. My investigations show that the movable

animals living at the surface of the ocean are all permanently or transitorily positively heliotropic (and also often negatively geotropic). Those among them that carry out the daily depth-migrations described above have some other peculiarities which we can only understand if we go somewhat deeper into the theory of animal heliotropism. We have already mentioned that there is a negative as well as a positive heliotropism: negatively heliotropic animals bring their median-plane into the direction of the rays of light, but turn their aboral pole toward the source of light. The difference in the behaviour of negatively and positively heliotropic animals is as follows: If light strikes one side of a positively heliotropic animal, an increase takes place in the tension of those muscles which turn the head to the source of light, while in the negatively heliotropic animal under the influence of one-sided illumination a decrease takes place in the tension of the same muscles. The result is that the negatively heliotropic animal is forced to move away from the source of light. Perhaps still another possibility should be considered here, namely, that the light aids the progressive movement when it strikes the oral end of a positively heliotropic animal, while it inhibits the progressive movement when it strikes the aboral end. The opposite may be true of negatively heliotropic animals. This would suggest a further analogy between heliotropism and galvanotropism.

Groom and I performed experiments on the larvæ

of *Balanus perforatus* which were known to make periodic depth-migrations (2). As one of our results, we found that these animals are sometimes negatively, sometimes positively heliotropic, and that we were able to make them positively or negatively heliotropic at desire. By weak light, especially gaslight, which contains comparatively few of the heliotropically effective blue rays, they became and remained positively heliotropic, while in strong light they soon became negatively heliotropic. This circumstance determines the periodic depth-migration of these animals. When they are near the surface of the ocean in the morning, the strong light makes them negatively heliotropic and forces them to go downwards vertically, because in the open sea only the vertical components of the reflected skylight have any effect. As soon as they approach a depth where the light is sufficiently weak, they become positively heliotropic. They must then begin to migrate upward again, but cannot reach the surface, because they soon come to a region where the light is so strong that they again become negatively heliotropic. Hence during the day they are held at a certain depth, which is, however, less than four hundred metres. But as soon as it becomes dark and the intensity of the light decreases more and more, they are forced to rise to higher regions on account of their positive heliotropism, until during the night, while the intensity of the light is weak, they are held at the surface of the water. Toward morning, when it begins to dawn, they again become negatively heliotropic and once more begin their downward migration. But the pelagic animals also show another depth-movement of a greater period, which corresponds more nearly with the migration of birds of passage. Chun has found that in the Bay of Naples during summer certain forms also remain at a greater depth during the night, never coming to the surface. This is probably due to the higher temperature which the surface of the water has in summer. I have found that certain animals, for instance, the larvæ of Polygordius, are positively heliotropic in a low temperature, while in a higher temperature they become negatively heliotropic (4).

I have also mentioned that geotropism also plays a part in these depth-migrations. The same circumstances which make the animals negatively heliotropic also make them positively geotropic, and *vice versa*. Thus I was able to show that in a low temperature the larvæ of Polygordius are also negatively geotropic, while in a high temperature they are positively geotropic (4). By means of this geotropism they are also forced in the dark to go to the surface when the temperature of the water is low. It is also probable that in many forms internal conditions similar to the nyctitropic phenomena in plants are influential in causing periodic depth-migrations.[1] We thus find that the migratory instinct, as far as it is

---

[1] This may account for the periodic migrations of certain animals (Medusæ) in polar regions. In such animals, changes in the specific gravity may take the place of heliotropic reactions.

expressed in the depth-migration of pelagic animals, is frequently determined by the presence of substances in the surfaces of the animal which are sensitive to light. These substances, however, produce different effects according to the intensity of the light or of the temperature (or perhaps according to internal conditions). They are further determined by the relations of symmetry of the animals. The central nervous system has nothing further to do with these phenomena than that it furnishes the protoplasmic connection between the skin and muscles. This disagrees with the centre theory of these instincts, but agrees with the segmental theory.

7. One might think that these ideas held good only for Invertebrates. Goltz has, however, made a remarkable discovery which seems to confirm the opinion that in Vertebrates the conditions are practically the same. A female dog that has given birth to a young one bites off the navel cord, licks the young, is very affectionate towards it, and allows no stranger to touch it. These motherly instincts are inherited, and there is no doubt that with the act of giving birth and the resulting processes in the sexual organs changes take place in the animal which make these instincts possible. One might think, especially in this case, of centres in the central nervous system which are stimulated directly through the nerves of the uterus. Now Goltz found that these instincts are also fully developed in dogs whose spinal cord is severed so far up that the stimuli from the uterus cannot reach the

brain (6). It is probable that certain substances which are developed during the pregnancy, birth, and lactation influence the character of the animal, just as certain poisons, for instance, alcohol, tobacco, or morphine, influence the reactions of a human being. It is of course possible that the sympathetic plays a part here, although this has been rendered improbable through the more recent experiments of Goltz and Ewald and of Ribbert.[1]

8. We have confined our attention to the simplest instincts, for these are best adapted for a complete analysis. Should we attempt a complete enumeration and discussion of instincts, we should have to devote several volumes to that subject alone. We should like to call attention to the conditions which are responsible for the fact that many instincts are difficult to analyse. One source of complication lies in the fact already mentioned, that changes in the condition of the blood, for example, those produced by metabolism, may change the forms of irritability and reaction. The young caterpillar of Porthesia is only heliotropic so long as it is starving, while it becomes indifferent to light as soon as it is fed. In plant-lice, the heliotropic irritability is connected with the growth of wings. The wingless forms may or may not show positive heliotropism; if we produce wings (by lowering the temperature or by letting the plant on which it lives dry out), the animal becomes energetically positively heliotropic. In ants heliotropism is more

[1] See next chapter.

intimately connected with the sexual development. I have never found true heliotropism in the workers, while the sexually mature males and females are decidedly positively heliotropic. Wherever these transitory changes of irritability are present, it requires experimental work to succeed in the analysis of the instinct.

A second series of difficulties arises from the influence of associative memory in many cases of instincts. The periodic depth-migration of marine animals is a simple case of instinctive migrations, while the migrations of birds or the accomplishments of the carrier-pigeon seem to be complicated by memory. It seems to be certain that the carrier-pigeon finds its way back by its visual memory of the locality from which it started. In the same way the migration of birds may be determined, if it is true that migrating birds return to their old nest. In the case of the birds, there is present in addition a purely inherited, instinctive element which causes restlessness at the time of migration. This restlessness and, perhaps to a certain extent, the direction of its flight are susceptible of a purely physiological analysis. The element of memory complicates many instinctive actions of wasps. I have had a chance to observe solitary wasps and am convinced that they find the way to their nest by means of the visual memory of the locality where it is situated. The same is apparently true of bees and possibly of ants. (See Chapter XV.)

9. The analysis of instincts from a purely physio-

logical point of view will ultimately furnish the data for a scientific ethics. Human happiness is based upon the possibility of a natural and harmonious satisfaction of the instincts.[1] One of the most important instincts is usually not even recognised as such, namely, the instinct of workmanship.[2] Lawyers, criminologists, and philosophers frequently imagine that only want makes man work. This is an erroneous view. We are instinctively forced to be active in the same way as ants or bees. The instinct of workmanship would be the greatest source of happiness if it were not for the fact that our present social and economic organisation allows only a few to satisfy this instinct. Robert Mayer has pointed out that any successful display or setting free of energy is a source of pleasure to us. This is the reason why the satisfaction of the instinct of workmanship is of such importance in the economy of life, for the play and learning of the child, as well as for the scientific or commercial work of the man.

10. We have finally to defend our physiological analysis of instincts against the reproach that it ignores the theory of evolution. In other words, it has been

[1] It is rather remarkable that we should still be under the influence of an ethics which considers the human instincts in themselves low and their gratification vicious. That such an ethics must have had a comforting effect upon the Orientals, whose instincts were inhibited or warped through the combined effects of an enervating climate, despotism, and miserable economic conditions, is intelligible, and it is perhaps due to a continuation of the unsatisfactory economic conditions that this ethics still prevails to some extent.

[2] I take this name from Veblen's book on *The Theory of the Leisure Class*, New York, 1899.

urged against us that instincts should be explained historically and not physiologically or causally. It seems to me that living organisms are machines and that their reactions can only be explained according to the same principles which are used by the physicist. Our ultimate aim in the analysis of instincts is to find out by which physical and chemical properties of protoplasm they are determined. Of course the physicist finds it useful to illustrate the mechanism of complicated machines by the comparison with simpler or older machines of the same kind. We have made use of this same method and heuristic principle by utilising in this book the reactions of simpler forms for the analysis of more complicated forms. Even if we were in possession of a scientific phylogeny instead of the fairy tales that go by that name at present, it would not relieve us of the task of explaining the instincts on the basis of the physical and chemical qualities of protoplasm.

11. At first sight it may seem a hopeless task to find a connection between the instinctive actions of animals and the properties of their protoplasm. And yet the task is not so great if we choose the right method. This method, in my opinion, consists in varying the instincts of an animal at desire. If we succeed in this we are able to find out how the physical qualities of protoplasm may affect the instincts. I have tried this in one case. A number of marine animals (Copepods, larvæ of Polygordius) which go away from the light can be forced to go to the light in two

ways, first by lowering the temperature, and second, by increasing the concentration of the sea-water (whereby the cells of the animals lose water). This instinct can again be reversed by raising the temperature or by lowering the concentration of the sea-water. Hence these instincts must depend upon such reversible changes in the material of the protoplasm as can be brought about by a loss of water or by a reduction of temperature. What these changes are can only be determined by further experiments. We find other instances where decrease in temperature has the same physiological effects as a loss of water. Plant-lice exist in wingless and in winged forms. We can at any time cause the growth of wings in the wingless forms by lowering the temperature or by letting the plant dry out (whereby the amount of water in the cells of plant-lice is reduced).[1]

BIBLIOGRAPHY.

1. LOEB, J. *Der Heliotropismus der Thiere und seine Uebereinstimmung mit dem Heliotropismus der Pflanzen.* Würzburg 1890.

2. GROOM and LOEB. *Der Heliotropismus der Nauplien von Balanus perforatus und die periodischen Tiefenwanderungen pelagischer Thiere.* *Biologisches Centralblatt*, Bd. x., 1890.

3. LOEB, J. *Ueber den Instinct und Willen der Thiere.* *Pflüger's Archiv*, Bd. xlvii., p. 407, 1890.

[1] I have found repeatedly that by the same conditions by which phenomena of growth and organisation can be controlled the instincts are controlled also. This indicates that there is a common basis for both classes of life phenomena. This common basis is the physical and chemical character of the mixture of substances which we call protoplasm.

4. LOEB, J. *Ueber künstliche Umwandlung positiv heliotropischer Thiere in negativ heliotropische und umgekehrt. Pflüger's Archiv*, Bd. liv., 1893.

5. LOEB, J. *On Egg Structure and the Heredity of Instincts. The Monist*, July, 1897.

6. GOLTZ, F. *Ueber den Einfluss des Nervensystems auf die Vorgänge während der Schwangerschaft und des Geburtsaktes. Pflüger's Archiv*, Bd. ix., 1874.

CHAPTER XIV

THE CENTRAL NERVOUS SYSTEM AND HEREDITY

1. The question as to how far the central nervous system comes into consideration for the processes of heredity is of great importance in educational problems. If we could hope that, as a result of the activity of a generation, its descendants would be born with a talent for this special activity, there would be a fertile field for the improvement of the human race. In order to decide this question, we must first turn our attention to those peculiarities which we know to be hereditary—namely, the form of the body and the instincts. The analysis of the instincts given in the previous chapter places us in a position to answer the question as to how they can be transmitted through the egg. All hereditary qualities of form, instincts, and reflexes must be transmitted through the sexual cells. The difficulty that appears is this : How can the sexual cells, which only represent a liquid mass enclosed in solid membranes, be the bearers of such apparently complicated structures as the forms that originate from them with their instincts and

reflexes? Either the apparent simplicity of the structure of the egg is only an illusion, and in reality the
structure of the egg is no less complicated than the
full-grown animal, or the sum of the elements which
we call the form and instincts of the full-grown animal is only the resultant of a few simpler elements
which can readily be transmitted through the egg
without its possessing a complicated structure. The
discussion of the mechanics of instincts in the last
chapter shows the latter to be the case. Let us consider those instincts that depend on heliotropic reactions—for instance, the flying of the moth into the
flame. This instinct is unequivocally determined, first,
by the presence of a substance in the surface of the
animal which is sensitive to light, and second, by the
symmetrical structure of the animal. For the transmission of a substance which is sensitive to light
through the egg no complicated mysterious structure
is necessary. Neither is a complicated structure
necessary for the egg in order that it may transmit
the symmetrical relations of the animal.

For the inheritance of form the conditions are not
very different. The egg is not the bearer of the form
of the full-grown animal, but of certain chemical substances, especially of ferments. According to the
stereochemical configuration of the latter, the products
of assimilation, and with these the materials of the
body, turn out differently. The process of development is not only a morphological but a chemical differentiation, and new combinations of substances are

continually formed from the original raw material. A further differentiation of the form may be and often is connected with every metabolic differentiation of the substance of the body. The results of experimental morphology harmonise entirely with this conception which was originated by Jaeger and Sachs, and which I have tried to develop in a series of articles. I will only mention the experiment in which the egg of the sea-urchin (Arbacia) was given the form of a double sphere, whereby each sphere developed into a complete sea-urchin. In this case it makes no difference whether the transformation of the sea-urchin into a double sphere takes place in the freshly fertilised egg or after the egg has already reached the 16- or 32-cell stage. These facts can only be understood if we think of the egg as nothing more than the bearer of *certain chemical* substances and not of mysterious morphological structures of a nature as complicated as that of the full-grown animal; and if we regard the morphological process of development only as a result or accompanying phenomenon of corresponding chemical transformations and physical changes. We may mention further in this connection that the processes of heteromorphosis—that is, the transformation or substitution of one organ for a morphologically different one by means of certain external influences—force us to the same view.

2. Tornier has developed a theory of the inheritance of acquired characters on the assumption of a new rôle of the central nervous system. According

to this theory, every change that takes place in the body is said to be accompanied by a corresponding change in the central nervous system. The changes in the central nervous system are then said to bring about a corresponding change in the egg. Thus, according to this theory, just as close a relation must exist between the central nervous system and the morphogenetic processes as between the central nervous system and the motor and sensory functions. It can readily be shown, however, that this assumption of Tornier goes much too far. When the larva of Amblystoma transforms itself into a sexually mature animal, it loses the gills which are located on the head and the tail-fins that are on the tail. Both organs disappear simultaneously. In a series of Amblystoma larvæ I severed the spinal cord in the vicinity of the shoulder-girdle. The parts of the animal before and behind the place of division are, as regards motor and sensory functions, like two separate animals. If the morphogenetic processes were as closely related to the central nervous system as the sensory and motor functions — as Tornier's theory demands — we should have expected that the gills and tail-fins would no longer be absorbed simultaneously, but at different times, just as in two different animals. *Without exception, in these animals with severed spinal cord the absorption of the head- and tail-organs occurred simultaneously* (1). In some of the animals operated upon, the change took place in a few days after the division, in others a longer interval elapsed. There can thus

be no doubt that the connection between the morphogenetic functions and the central nervous system is
much more slight than between this organ and the
sensory and motor functions.

I am inclined to believe that the simultaneous dis-
appearance of gills and tail-fins is due to some change
occurring in the blood,—*e. g.*, the appearance of certain
enzymes, or possibly changes in the number of red
blood corpuscles, etc.

It has been urged that in this experiment the sympathetic system transmitted the connection between the
two halves of the animal. The sympathetic has
always been used as a bridge across the gulf between
preconceived notions and facts. I am pretty certain
that at least in a number of my Amblystomas the sympathetic was cut. But as I did not make sure of this
I will not urge this point. But I may at least point
out the true reliability of this bridge. It had been a
generally accepted belief that the secretory activity
of the milk glands during and after pregnancy was
caused by the stimulation of the nerve-endings of the
uterus. Goltz severed the spinal cord in the pectoral
region of a female dog which afterwards became pregnant and gave birth to young ones. It turned out
that the mammary glands in front and behind the place
of the section began to secrete milk equally well.
Goltz concluded that the secretion was not due to a
nervous influence. As was to be expected, those who
try to explain everything by the omnipotence of the
central nervous system at once pointed out that the

sympathetic connected the two halves of the spinal cord in Goltz's dog. Recently Ribbert made an experiment which, if correct, does away with these mysterious sympathetic influences (8). He transplanted a milk gland to the ear of a guinea-pig. The guinea-pig became pregnant and the gland on the ear began to secrete. It is evident that a change in the blood or lymph must be responsible for the secretion of milk glands during pregnancy, possibly the appearance of certain enzymes.

Schaper has added an experiment that speaks for the lack of dependence of the morphogenetic development on the central nervous system. In a tadpole six mm. long he extirpated the brain and the medulla oblongata. When the animal was killed seven days later, the spinal cord seemed to have vanished. Nevertheless the healing of the wound, growth, and development continued during the seven days (2). In face of the fact that the first processes of development precede the formation of the central nervous system in every animal, these results need not surprise us. They suffice, however, to convince us that the processes of development and the formation of organs are less closely connected with the central nervous system than the sensory and motor processes. For this reason we cannot well decide in favour of the assumption that every impression on the central nervous system must impart itself to the egg, with which it is, moreover, not connected.

3. But how shall we make the fact that certain

mental diseases are hereditary harmonise with this view? It is, perhaps, not impossible that those mental diseases that are hereditary are, in reality, chemical diseases caused by poisons that are formed in the body just as special substances, for instance, alcohol, hashish, and other intoxicating substances, produce temporary mental diseases (3). The delirium of fever as well as certain other mental diseases may owe their origin to poisons which are formed in the body. It is quite possible that these poisons are also formed in the normal body. It is only necessary that they be formed in somewhat larger quantities or destroyed in somewhat smaller quantities in the body of the insane than in the normal man. It is further not at all necessary that these hypothetical poisons which cause mental diseases be formed in the central nervous system. They may be formed in any organ of the body. It is only necessary that they affect the central nervous system — in other words, that they be nerve-poisons.

Nothing is better qualified to make this view clear than the result which the destruction of the thyroid gland has on the mental and physical development of children. We know that in case of degeneration of the thyroid gland the growth and mental development of children are retarded. Idiocy may result from the destruction of the thyroid gland. It has been found that an improvement or even a cure can be attained by feeding patients afflicted with this trouble with the thyroid substance of animals. Baumann found that the thyroid gland contains an element which is contained in no other organ of the body, namely, iodine. It is thus conceivable that hereditary mental diseases are chemical diseases. The germ-cells may in these diseases also be influenced by the poisons circulating in the blood.

4. If we thus deny the *immediate* influence of the central nervous system on the germ, and assume a chemical theory of heredity, it might still be possible that the central nervous system could influence heredity indirectly, in so far as it can affect the chemical processes of the body. As illustrations of a chemical effect of the nerves, the fact is mentioned that stimulation of the nerves of certain glands produces a secretion. Mathews has shown, however, that in cases where stimulation of the sympathetic produces a secretion, the glands contain muscular fibres which contract when stimulated, and in this way press a liquid out of the ducts (4). (Conditions seem to be different in the case of the secretion produced by stimulation of the chorda, but it is also possible that in this case the secretion is only an *indirect* effect of the stimulation caused by changes in the circulation.) There are other cases of an apparent chemical effect of the nerves. The fact that herpes zoster follows the nerves has led many to assume that this disease is caused by a trophical influence of the nerves. But we know that in the case of rabies the micro-organism or the poison creeps along the nerves. Goltz has found that ulcerations and suppurations occur on the skin behind the cut after division of the spinal cord, which are so sym-

metrical that it is impossible to attribute them solely to external injuries. They occur only during the first weeks after the operation, disappearing later on (5). It is conceivable that the cause of these phenomena is to be sought in abnormal chemical processes which are perhaps caused by the vasomotor nerves in so far as disturbances in the supply of oxygen, etc., are determined by them. These disturbances occasionally fail to appear. Physicians are familiar with these phenomena of bed-sores which ensue after lesion of the spinal cord. One fact that Goltz and Ewald found is especially interesting for the theory of these processes. When they severed the spinal cord of animals, these phenomena of ulceration of the skin were very pronounced. But if they afterward operated on the spinal cord behind the cut, the disturbances were much less severe or failed to appear. Thus the separation of a part of the spinal cord from the brain is accompanied by more serious consequences than the subsequent destruction of the spinal cord itself (5).

An inflammation of the cornea occurs generally after the division of the trigeminus of the same side. This inflammation is naturally caused by bacteria, but the fact that these bacteria affect the cornea whose sensory nerve is severed might have two causes: either the animal on account of the lack of sensibility might not notice the foreign bodies (dust, etc.) that get into the eye and cause a wound, or as a result of the division of the nerve changes take place in the cornea which render it more susceptible to inflam-

14

mation. The latter might be the case if Gaule's statement is correct, namely, that histological changes can be shown in the cornea ten minutes after the division of the trigeminus (6, 7). In this case it can only be that the power of resistance or, more accurately speaking, the chemical nature of the tissue is changed as a result of the lesion of the nerve. If this be true, it does not force us to the assumption of specific trophic nerves; if it is true that the influence of every nervous impulse on the affected tissue is chemical, all nerves are in one sense trophic, and it would be quite erroneous to maintain that certain nerves serve trophic functions exclusively while others are sensory and motor. There are no specifically trophic nerves, but it is possible that many nerves produce indirectly (for instance, through disturbances of the circulation and limitation of the supply of oxygen) such extensive chemical changes that morphological changes of the tissue ensue.

If this is in reality the case, a possibility still exists that the central nervous system also affects the sexual cells indirectly, in so far as disturbances of circulation and hence chemical changes are produced, which may modify the sexual cells contained in the testes and ovaries chemically. Thus there might be a very remote chance that brain-activity of one generation might lead to the formation of chemical substances which affect the sexual cells. It is difficult to understand, however, what should cause these sexual cells to produce descendants with greater intellect. The intellect is not proportional to chemical changes, like muscular activity. In the brain of an idiot and of a genius the same chemical changes may occur. The difference between the two, however, is that the idiot fails to notice valuable associations of ideas while the brain of the genius retains them. We arrive thus at the conclusion that a transmission of hereditary characteristics through the egg is only possible in the form of specific chemical substances, and that the central nervous system could only influence heredity, if it could bring about the formation of special substances in the egg (by influencing metabolism). It would, of course, first have to be proved that the central nervous system has such an influence upon the sexual cells, and this is extremely doubtful. For this reason we should not be justified in maintaining that the activity of a generation can produce an hereditary increase of the ability and tendencies in the same direction. Herbert Spencer gives as a proof of this last possibility the fact that the circles of touch in the tip of our tongue are the smallest. He believes that this is due to the fact that from time immemorial man had the tendency to examine the spaces between the teeth with the tongue, and this is supposed to have caused an hereditary increase in the nerve-endings of the tongue. Spencer overlooks the fact that in the tip of the nose the circles of touch are also a comparative minimum, and it is certain that this organ has not been used for such a purpose since time immemorial.

It is more probable that the relative number of the nerve-endings or, more correctly speaking, the relative size of the circles of touch in the tip of the tongue and the tip of the nose is determined by the relatively small radius of curvature or the minimal areal growth of these tips.

BIBLIOGRAPHY.

1. LOEB, J. *Hat das Centralnervensystem einen Einfluss auf die Vorgänge der Larvenmetamorphose? Archiv für Entwickelungsmechanik*, Bd. iv., 1896.

2. SCHAPER, A. *Experimental Studies on the Influence of the Central Nervous System upon the Development of the Embryo. Journal of the Boston Soc. of Medical Science*, Jan., 1898.

3. MEYER, ADOLF. *A Short Sketch of the Problems of Psychiatry. Am. Jour. of Insanity*, vol. liii., 1897.

4. MATHEWS, A. *The Physiology of Secretion. Annals N. Y. Acad. of Science*, vol. xi., No. 14, 1898.

5. GOLTZ and EWALD. *Der Hund mit verkürztem Rückenmark. Pflüger's Arch.*, Bd. lxiii., 1896.

6. GAULE, J. *Der Einfluss des Trigeminus auf die Hornhaut. Physiologisches Centralblatt*, Bd. v., 1891.

7. GAULE, J. *Wie beherrscht der Trigeminus die Ernährung der Hornhaut. Physiologisches Centralblatt*, Bd. vi., 1892.

8. RIBBERT, H. *Ueber Transplantation von Ovarium, Hoden und Mamma. Arch. f. Entwickelungsmechanik*, vol. vii., 1898.

CHAPTER XV

THE DISTRIBUTION OF ASSOCIATIVE MEMORY IN THE ANIMAL KINGDOM

1. The most important problem in the physiology of the central nervous system is the analysis of the mechanisms which give rise to the so-called psychic phenomena. The latter appear, invariably, as a function of an elementary process, namely, the activity of the associative memory. By associative memory I mean the two following peculiarities of our central nervous system : First, that processes which occur there leave an impression or trace by which they can be reproduced even under different circumstances than those under which they originated. This peculiarity can be imitated by machines like the phonograph. Of course, we have no right to assume that the traces of processes in the central nervous system are analogous to those in the phonograph. The second peculiarity is, that two processes which occur simultaneously or in quick succession will leave traces which fuse together, so that if later one of the processes is repeated, the other will necessarily be repeated also. The odour of a rose will at the same

time reproduce its visual image in our memory, or, even more than that, it will reproduce the recollection of scenes or persons who were present when the same odour made its first strong impression on us. By associative memory we mean, therefore, that mechanism by means of which a stimulus produces not only the effects which correspond to its nature and the specific structure of the stimulated organ, but which produces, in addition, such effects of other causes as at some former time may have attacked the organism almost or quite simultaneously with the given stimulus (2). The chief problem of the physiology of the brain is, then, evidently this : What is the physical character of the mechanism of associative memory ? As we said in the first chapter, the answer to this question will probably be found in the field of physical chemistry.

I think it can be shown that what the metaphysician calls consciousness are phenomena determined by the mechanism of associative memory. Mach has pointed out that the consciousness of self or the ego is simply a phrase for the fact that certain constituents of memory are constantly or more frequently produced than others (1, 11). The complex of these elements of memory is the " ego " or the " soul," or the personality of the metaphysicians. To a certain extent we are able to enumerate these constituents. They are the visual image of the body so far as it lies in the field of vision, certain sensations of touch which are repeated very frequently, the sound of our own voice, certain interests and cares, a certain feeling of comfort or discomfort according to temperament or state of health, etc. (1, 11).

An inventory of all the memory-constituents of the ego-complex of different persons would show that the consciousness of self is not a definite unit, but, as Mach maintains, merely an artificial separation of those constituents of memory which occur most frequently in our perceptions. These will necessarily be subject to considerable variation in the same person in the different periods of life.

If we speak of loss or an interruption of consciousness, we mean a loss or an interruption of the activity of associative memory. If a faint is caused directly by lack of oxygen or indirectly by a disturbance in the circulatory system, the activity of associative memory ceases. This was proved by Speck's experiments on the effects of a low pressure of oxygen. When he breathed air with less than eight per cent. of oxygen, he soon fainted. In these experiments, he had to count the number of respirations. Before he fainted, he became confused in his counting and forgot what happened. When this disturbance in counting began to appear, he knew it was time to discontinue the experiment. When a loss of consciousness is produced by narcotics or anæsthetics, we·have again to deal with an interruption in the activity of the associative memory. It is the same in the case of a deep sleep.

The metaphysician speaks of conscious sensations and conscious will. That the will is only a function of the mechanism of the associative memory can be proved. We speak of conscious volition if an idea of the resulting final complex of sensations is present before the movements causing it have taken place or have ceased. In volition three processes occur. The one is an innervation of some kind which may be caused directly or indirectly by an external stimulus. This process of innervation produces two kinds of effects. The one effect is the activity of the associative memory which produces the sensations that in former cases accompanied or followed the same innervation. The second effect is a coördinated muscular activity. It happens that in such cases the reaction-time for the memory-effect of the innervation is shorter than the time for the muscular effect. When some internal process causes us to open the window, the activity of the associative memory produces the idea of sensations which will follow or accompany the opening of the window sooner than the act of opening really occurs. As we do not realise this any more than we realise the inverted character of the retina-image, we consider the memory-effect of the innervation as the cause of the muscular effect. The common cause of both effects, the innervating process, escapes our immediate observation as our senses do not perceive it. The will of the metaphysicians is then clearly the outcome of an illusion due to the necessary incompleteness of self-observation. Our conception of will harmonises with Münsterberg's and James's views on this subject (6, 12). I think that we are justified in substituting the term activity of associative memory for the phrase consciousness used by the metaphysicians.

2. We have spoken of *associative* memory because the word *memory* is often applied in quite a different sense scientifically, namely, to signify any after-effect of external circumstances. For instance, the term memory has been used to account for the fact that a plant which had been cultivated in the tropics will often not endure low temperatures so well as a plant of the same species which was raised in the north. It is true in this case that preceding conditions influence the ability of the plant to react, but the process differs from the one which we have called associative memory in the lack of associative processes. No definite stimulus produces in a plant, in addition to its own effects, those of another entirely different stimulus which at some former time occurred simultaneously with the given stimulus. It is probable that the tropical plant is somewhat different chemically from the plant raised in the north. This would account for its smaller power of resistance. Further illustrations of a different use of the word memory can easily be given.

Many moths sleep during the day and wake in the evening when it becomes dark. If kept for days in a dark room, they will continue at first to do the same thing. The same is true of certain plants. One might also say in this case that the moth or the plant "remembers" the difference between day and night. It is probable, however, that internal changes take place in the organism, corresponding to the periodic change of day and night, and that these changes continue for a time in the same periodicity, when the animal is kept in the dark.

3. We will then consider the extent of associative memory in the animal kingdom instead of the extent of consciousness among animals. How can we determine whether an animal possesses the mechanism necessary for associative memory? The criteria for the existence of associative memory must form the basis of a future comparative psychology. It will require more observations than we have made at present to give absolutely unequivocal criteria. For the present, we can say that if an animal can learn, that is, if it can be trained to react in a desired way upon certain stimuli (signs), it must possess associative memory. The only fault with this criterion lies in the fact that an animal may be able to remember (and to associate) and yet may not yield to our attempts to train it. In this case other experiments must be substituted which will prove that the animal does associate or remember.

We may conclude that associative memory is present when an animal responds upon hearing its name called, or when it can be trained upon hearing a certain sound to go to the place where it is usually fed. The optical stimulus of the place where the food is to be found and the sensations of hunger and satiety are not qualitatively the same, but they occur simultaneously in the animal. The fusion or growing together of heterogeneous but by chance simultaneous processes is a sure criterion for the existence of associative memory (2).

Associative memory probably exists in most mammals. The dog which comes when its name is called, which runs away from the whip, which welcomes its master joyfully, has associative memory. In birds, it is likewise present. The parrot learns to talk ; the dove finds its way home. In lower Vertebrates, memory is also occasionally found. Tree-frogs, for example, can be trained, upon hearing a sound, to go to a certain place for food. In other frogs, *Rana esculenta*, for instance, no reaction is as yet known which proves the existence of associative memory. Some fishes evidently possess memory ; in sharks, however, its existence is doubtful. With regard to the Invertebrates, the question is difficult to determine. The statements of enthusiasts who discover consciousness and resemblance to man on every side should not be too readily accepted.

4. In my experiments on the tropisms of animals, it became clear to me how easy it is for an observer who is inclined to think anthropomorphically to regard machine-like effects of external stimuli on lower animals as the expression of intelligence. He needs only to neglect the analysis of the external stimuli. I have protested against the anthropomorphisms of Romanes, Eimer, Preyer, and others in a series of articles (2, 3). Bethe has recently published a paper on the psychic qualities of ants and bees in which he took special pains not to fall into the gross anthropo-

morphisms which have characterised this field heretofore (4). But I am afraid that he went too far
and that he overlooked the fact that bees and ants
possess associative memory. Bethe assumes associative memory as the criterion for the existence of consciousness, as I had done before. (He has evidently
overlooked, or at least does not mention, my work on
this subject.) According to him: "An animal that
is able to do the same things the first day of its existence which it can do at the end of its life, that learns
nothing, that always reacts in the same way upon
the same stimulus, possesses no consciousness." This
statement is not sufficient. It is possible that an animal at birth, or just after hatching, may not be fully
developed. In this case it may be able later to perform actions which would have been impossible
on the first day, without possessing associative memory. Yet according to Bethe's definition such actions
would indicate associative memory.

It is a well-known fact that if an ant be removed
from a nest and afterwards put back it will not be
attacked, while almost invariably an ant belonging to
another nest will be attacked. It has been customary
to use the words memory, enmity, friendship, in describing this fact. Now Bethe made the following
experiment. An ant was placed in the liquids (blood
and lymph) squeezed out from the bodies of nest
companions and was then put back into its nest; it
was not attacked. It was then put in the juice taken
from the inmates of a "hostile" nest and was at once

attacked and killed. Hence chemical stimuli of certain volatile substances will excite the ants. In this case we do not need to assume intelligence any more than we do in the case of the tentacles of Actinians which, as we have seen, will immediately carry a piece of filter paper soaked in meat-juice to the mouth while they ignore a piece of paper soaked in sea-water. The assumption of machine-like irritable structures is quite sufficient here to explain the reaction. Memory is quite unnecessary. Possibly the behaviour of the ant may be explained in the same way. Bethe was able to prove by special experiments that these reactions of ants are not learned by experience, but are inherited. The "knowing" of "friend and foe" among ants is thus reduced to different reactions, depending upon the nature of the chemical stimulus and in no way depending upon memory.

Memory and intellect are supposed to be responsible for the fact that an ant is able to find its way back to the nest and that when "foragers" have discovered honey or sugar the other ants of the nest soon go to it in great numbers. The ability to communicate information was assumed in this case. Bethe, however, was able to determine by means of ingenious experiments that an ant, when taking a new direction from the nest for the first time, always returns by the same path. This shows that some trace must be left behind which serves as a guide back to the nest. If the ant returning by this path bear no spoils, Bethe found that no other ants try this direction. But if it bring back honey or sugar, other ants are sure to try the path. Hence something of the substances carried over this path by the ants must remain on the path.. These substances must be strong enough to affect the ants chemically. I can prove by the following observation, which must surely have been made before me by many breeders of butterflies, that Bethe is justified in the assumption that insects are affected by extremely weak chemical stimuli. I placed a female butterfly of a certain species in a cigar-box, and closed the box. The box was then suspended half way between the ceiling and floor of the room and then the window was opened. At first no butterfly of this species was visible far or near. In less than half an hour a male butterfly of the same species appeared on the street. When it reached the height of the window, its flight was retarded and it came gradually toward the window. It flew into the room and soon up to the cigar-box, upon which it perched. During the afternoon, two other males of the same species came to the box. Thus we see that butterflies and certainly many other insects possess a delicacy of chemical irritability which, if possible, is finer than that of the best blood-hound. Plateau maintains that insects are attracted to the flowers by the odour rather than by the colour and marking. The dioptric apparatus of insects is very inferior to that of the human eye, while their chemical irritability is much superior to that of our olfactory epithelium. I believe that both odour and colour may influence insects.

One of the most remarkable conclusions of Bethe
is the assumption that the roads of the ants have two
paths which differ chemically from each other, one
leading from and one toward the nest. Bethe tried
to prove this by experiments that had been undertaken
before by Lubbock, who obtained no definite results.
Bethe arranged a broad ant-street so that it led over
a turn-bridge. He revolved this bridge 180°, when
the ants were passing to and from the nest, and found
that it was impossible for the two armies to continue
on their way. He again turned the bridge 180° so
that the tracks had the original orientation. The
ants continued in the direction they were pursuing
when disturbed. An observation made by Forel also
agrees with this: "An ant that is picked up from
the path while moving and then put down again is almost sure to take the same direction, no matter what
orientation is given to its body." This, however,
only holds good for a street which is often travelled.
A weak track which leads in one direction is qualified
to lead in the opposite direction, as is shown by the
fact that an ant which has found a new supply returns
to the nest the same way that it came. It is evidently
the load and lack of load which determine which path
the ant will take (that is, to or from the nest). The
load causes the ant to go to the nest reflexly; the lack
of a load causes it to go from the nest. Bethe comes
to the conclusion that the reactions of ants, which
have always been considered psychic phenomena, are
merely reflex processes comparable to the tropisms.

5. Although I heartily sympathise with Bethe's re-action against the anthropomorphic conception of animal instincts, I yet believe that he is mistaken in denying the existence of associative memory in ants or bees. The fact that bees find their way home through the air cannot depend upon any trace left in their path. It can only depend upon memory and, as I believe, upon visual memory. If the bee-hive be removed while the bees have swarmed out, they will return to and gather at the spot where the entrance to the hive used to be. Bethe is not willing to admit that this indicates the existence of a visual image of memory of the locality of the nest, professing to consider it possible that unknown forces guide the bee reflexly.

I have recently had a chance to observe the activity of solitary wasps and have come to the conclusion that these animals are guided back to their nest by their memory.

My observations were made on Ammophila, a species of wasps, whose habits have been carefully studied and described by Mr. and Mrs. Peckham (7). Ammophila makes a small hole in the ground and then goes out to hunt for a caterpillar, which, when found, it paralyses by one or several stings. The wasp carries the caterpillar back to the nest, puts it into the hole, and covers it with sand. Before this is done, it deposits its egg and the caterpillar serves the young larva as food.

I will describe one observation on the means these

wasps employ of finding their way to the nest, which absolutely excludes the assumption that they are guided reflexly by known or unknown stimuli, and which indicates that they find their way through memory. An Ammophila had a hole in a flower-bed in my front yard. The wasp, of course, left the yard flying. Towards noon I saw an Ammophila running on the sidewalk of the street in front of the yard carrying a caterpillar in its mouth. The weight of the caterpillar prevented it from flying. The yard is separated from the street by a cemented stone wall. I noticed that the wasp repeatedly made an attempt to climb upon the wall, but kept falling down. Suspecting that it might have its nest in the yard I was curious to see whether and how it would find the nest.

It followed the wall until it reached the neighbouring yard, which had no wall. It now left the street and crept into this yard. Then crawling through the fence which separated the two yards, it dropped the caterpillar near the foot of a tree, and flew away. After a short zigzag flight it alighted on a flower-bed in which I noticed two holes. It soon left the bed and flew back to the tree, not in a straight line but in three stages, stopping twice on its way. At the third stop it landed at the place where the caterpillar lay. The caterpillar was then dragged to the hole, pulled into it, and covered with sand.

As the wasp only walks to the hole when carrying a caterpillar, it is impossible to say that it followed a

15

trace and was guided reflexly when it carried the caterpillar to the nest. The repeated attempts to climb the wall of the yard which first attracted my attention indicate that the wasp remembered the location of the nest. The fact that it returned to fetch the caterpillar indicates that it remembered having dropped it, and also where it had been dropped. The zigzag character of its flight shows that it was not guided reflexly.

While these animals without doubt possess associative memory they possess little "intelligence."

I mentioned that the Ammophila covered the hole in which it had buried the caterpillar. In order to cover it, the wasp had to pick up little grains of sand in the neighbourhood of the hole and carry them in its mandibles to the hole. Once, while it had its back turned to the nest and was picking up a grain of sand, I covered the hole with a clover blossom. The wasp was no longer able to find the hole. It ran and flew about in the most excited manner, returning each time to the place where the hole had been, without being able to discover it. I finally removed the flower, and the wasp immediately found the hole and continued covering it with sand. The blossom with which I covered the hole weighed considerably less than the caterpillar which the wasp carried with such ease between its mandibles. The fact that the wasp kept returning to the spot where the hole was, indicates again the existence of memory in these animals.

Bethe's conclusions have been criticised by Wasmann (8) as far as ants, and by von Buttel-Reepen (9) as far as bees, are concerned. I think that bees and ants possess associative memory. In their reactions, however, reflex or instinctive elements and memory elements are mixed together. The task remains to discover how much of a rôle associative memory plays in the various habits of bees, ants, and wasps.

6. The possibility of associative memory must be conceded in the case of spiders, certain Crustacea, and Cephalopods, but it is in all probability wanting in Cœlenterates and in worms. We saw that Actinians refuse water-soaked paper wads and take meat, though *our* organs of taste cannot distinguish between the two. Some authors would have called this an expression of intelligence because the Actinian can "discriminate" and "make a selection." According to this, consciousness and intelligence should be attributed to the chemical elements, for they unite only with certain other elements. The term "power of discrimination" is often merely an ill-chosen expression for the fact that different causes have different effects. This difference of the effects may in some cases depend on associative memory, but in order to find out these cases we must first prove that the forms under consideration have associative memory. In Actinians, however, all attempts to prove the existence of associative memory have been fruitless. This is shown in the experiments on Cerianthus mentioned above, in which I succeeded in producing, below the

normal head, a second head, which had an oral disc and tentacles but no mouth (Fig. 12, p. 52). The tentacles never learned that no mouth was present, but continued when meat was offered to make the attempt to force it into an opening that did not exist.

Some reactions of lower animals cannot be repeated indefinitely. We must not conclude, however, that this is due to processes of association and that the animal has learned certain effects. It is a well-known fact that many worms that live in cases suddenly withdraw into their cases when a shadow is cast on them. I analysed this process and showed that the shadow has nothing to do with the phenomenon. It is due to a reaction against negative variations in the intensity of the light, comparable to the "break-contraction" of a muscle. The experiment does not succeed if repeated an indefinite number of times in succession. Nagel concludes from this that these worms possess "the ability to judge." "The animal recognises that the shadow cast so frequently does not signify the approach of an enemy or of any other danger" (Nagel). In reality these reactions are inherited forms of irritability that have nothing to do with experience. The reason that the reaction ceases if repeated frequently is due to a simple after-effect of the stimulus, a case that we often meet in the physiology of both animals and plants. The assumption that such low animals as eyeless worms and snails possess ideas or even the one idea of "an approaching enemy or other impending danger" is entirely arbitrary. Graber also maintained that animals that go to the light do so because they love it, and another author thought that animals fly into the flame out of curiosity. It is not worth while to follow up such anthropomorphisms in the biological literature. Biology is as much justified in ignoring them as modern physics is in ignoring the fact that savages explain the locomotive by supposing a horse to be concealed within it. On the contrary, biology should concern itself with a systematic investigation of the different animals in regard to the existence of associative memory. The total results of such an investigation will furnish the material for a future comparative psychology.

7. Our conception meets with an apparent difficulty in the fact that stimuli which call forth sensations of pain in us produce also reactions in lower animals which have no memory. These reactions are naturally regarded as the expression of sensations of pain. The injured worm writhes and wriggles, and it is difficult to rid ourselves of the impression that these movements are the expression of severe pain. Yet W. W. Norman proved that this conclusion is by no means justified (5, 10). He found that if an earthworm is divided transversely, only the posterior piece makes these writhing movements, while the anterior piece crawls off as if nothing had happened. It would, of course, be absurd to assume that the posterior piece alone is capable of a sensation of pain, while the anterior piece, which contains the brain,

experiences no such sensation. If we continue the experiment and divide the posterior piece in the middle, the anterior part crawls off calmly while the posterior part again makes writhing movements. We obtain the same results if we divide the anterior piece. No matter how the worm is divided, the piece in front of the place of division shows coördinated crawling movements, while the piece behind the place of division makes writhing movements. It is not even necessary to cut the worm. If we only touch it with the point of a pencil the posterior part wriggles, the anterior part elongates. The only conclusion that can be drawn is that the stimulus of cutting produces a different effect when it extends forward through the worm, from the effect which it produces when it extends backward. The movements do not indicate that the animal possesses sensations of pain.

Similar observations can be made in other Annelids. In Planarians I had already observed that they give no evidence of pain when they are divided transversely. The forward piece crawls or swims as if nothing had happened, occasionally merely hastening its movements.

But even in insects and Crustaceans pieces can be cut off without any reaction from the animal which might be interpreted as the expression of a pain-sensation.

Janet has observed that the abdomen of a bee can be cut off while the bee is sucking honey without causing any interruption in its occupation. In 1888 I noticed something similar in a small Crustacean, Gammarus, during copulation. The abdomen of the male can be cut off while it is seated on the female without causing it to release the female. In fact, unless my memory deceives me, these males without abdomen, when torn away from the female, were ready to hold another as soon as they could find one. Norman has added a great many similar observations on insects and Crustaceans (10). The result of all these observations is that either these Invertebrates do not react to injury in a way which indicates the existence of pain-sensation, or that, if there seem to be such reactions, they do not justify the assumption of the existence of pain-sensations.

We cannot be surprised that among those representatives of the lower Vertebrates which have no associative memory, or only traces of it, similar conditions exist.

Hermann and other physiologists maintain that the reactions of lower Vertebrates under the influence of an ascending current are due to pain-sensations, while the descending current is said to have a soothing effect. Garrey and I came to the conclusion that, in both cases, different sets of muscles were thrown into activity (see Chapter XI.). In order to test Hermann's view, we experimented on larvæ of Amblystoma whose spinal cord had been cut between the head and the tail-end of the body. We found that in the ascending current only the tail-end of the animal showed those reactions which Hermann and the other physiologists had considered as the expression of pain-sensations. I may mention further that when the motions following the stimulation of the semicircular canals were first observed they were considered by some authors as the expression of pain-sensations.

Norman observed that sharks and flounders react in no way against very severe operations, *e. g.*, the laying bare of the semicircular canals, provided that respiration was not interfered with (10). As soon as the water-supply to the mouth was cut off, they made violent motions, which are characteristic for the condition of beginning asphyxiation and which have nothing in common with conscious acts. Sharks and flounders belong to that class of Vertebrates which have practically no associative memory.

It therefore seems to me that our experience concerning the pain-sensations of animals does not contradict our view regarding the limits of associative memory or the consciousness of the metaphysicians.

Of course I do not expect to convince the sentimentalists and Darwinians. The former will say that their "feeling" tells them that an earthworm is capable of pain-sensations. My reply to these is that the burden of proof rests upon them. If a person maintains that there is a gaseous Vertebrate in the air it is plainly his duty to prove its existence, and not the duty of all the other scientists to disprove it. Otherwise we might be called upon to waste our lives in disproving the statements of any insane person or impostor. The Darwinians will doubt the possibility that pain-sensations or any definite characters should appear in certain forms without existing (although in a rudimentary form) in the whole animal kingdom. To these we shall reply in the next chapter (p. 251).

8. At the end of the chapter on instincts we mentioned that in those animals which possess associative memory the instinctive reactions may be modified or complicated by the influence of the associations. This influence can be so powerful that the instincts are warped or suppressed altogether. By education and experience the memory of man is filled with a number of associations which can inhibit any reflex or instinctive motor process. To a certain extent these inhibitory associations are necessary for the preservation of the life of the individual. Moreover, it is necessary to provide the child with associations which prevent "dissipation," *e. g.*, the cultivation of one or a few instincts at the expense of others. The greatest happiness in life can be obtained only if all the instincts—that of workmanship included— can be maintained at a certain optimal intensity. But while it is certain that the individual can ruin or diminish the value of its life by a one-sided development of its instincts — *e. g.*, dissipation,—it is at the same time true that the economic and social conditions can ruin or diminish the value of life for a great number of individuals.[1]

[1] It is no doubt true that in our present social and economic condition more than ninety per cent. of human beings lead an existence whose value is far below what it should be. They are compelled by want to sacrifice a number of instincts, especially the most valuable among them, that of workmanship, in

Although we recognise no metaphysical free-will, we do not deny personal responsibility. We can fill the memory of the young generation with such associations as will prevent wrongdoing or dissipation. If in a human being such associations are lacking, it points to an organic deficiency or to an insufficient education, for which in some cases the parents, in the majority of cases, our present social conditions, are responsible.

Punishment is, perhaps, justifiable in so far as it may bring about inhibitory associations or may be able to strengthen the inhibitory associations of weaker members of society. Inhibitions to be effective, however, must be cultivated in youth, as the time at which the penal code is enforced is usually too late for any lasting benefit. Cruelty in the penal code and the tendency to exaggerate punishments are sure signs of a low civilisation and of an imperfect educational system.

order to save the lowest and most imperative, that of eating. If those who amass immense fortunes could possibly intensify their own lives with their abundance, it might perhaps be rational to let many suffer in order to have a few cases of true happiness. But for an increase of happiness only that amount of money is of service which can be used for the harmonious development and satisfaction of inherited instincts. For this comparatively little is necessary. The rest is of no more use to a man than the surplus of oxygen in the atmosphere. As a matter of fact, the only true satisfaction a multi-millionaire can possibly get from increasing his fortune, is the satisfaction of the instinct of workmanship, or the pleasure that is connected with a successful display of energy. The scientist gets this satisfaction without diminishing the value of life of his fellow-beings, and the same should be true for the business man.

BIBLIOGRAPHY.

1. MACH, E. *Contributions to the Analysis of the Sensations.* The Open Court Publishing Co., Chicago, 1897.

2. LOEB, J. *Beiträge zur Gehirnphysiologie der Würmer. Pflüger's Archiv*, Bd. lvi., 1894. *Zur Psychologie und Physiologie der Aktinien. Pflüger's Archiv*, Bd. lix., 1896. *Zur Theorie der physiologischen Licht- und Schwerkraftwirkungen. Pflüger's Archiv*, Bd. lxvi., 1897.

3. LOEB, J. *Weitere Bemerkungen über den Heliotropismus der Thiere und seine Uebereinstimmung mit dem Heliotropismus der Pflanzen. Plüger's Archiv*, Bd. xlvii.

4. BETHE, A. *Dürfen wir den Ameisen und den Bienen psychische Qualitäten zuschreiben? Pflüger's Archiv*, Bd. lxx., 1898.

5. NORMAN, W. W. *Dürfen wir aus den Reactionen niederer Thiere auf Schmerzempfindungen derselben schliessen? Pflüger's Archiv*, Bd. lxvii., 1897.

6. MÜNSTERBERG, H. *Die Willenshandlung.* Freiburg, 1888.

7. PECKHAM, G. W. and E. G. *On the Instincts and Habits of the Solitary Wasps. Wisconsin Geological and Natural History Survey,* 1898.

8. WASMANN, E. *Die psychischen Fähigkeiten der Ameisen. Zoologica,* vol. xi., 1899.

9. v. BUTTEL-REEPEN. *Sind die Bienen Reflexmaschinen? Biologisches Centralblatt,* vol. xx., 1900.

10. NORMAN, W. W. *Do the Reactions of the Lower Animals against Injury Indicate Pain-Sensations? The American Journ. of Physiology,* vol. iii., 1900.

11. MACH, E. *Die Analyse der Empfindungen und das Verhältniss des Physischen zum Psychischen.* Jena, 1900.

12. JAMES, W. *The Principles of Psychology.* New York, 1890.

CHAPTER XVI

CEREBRAL HEMISPHERES AND ASSOCIATIVE MEMORY

1. The view that consciousness is only a metaphysical term for the phenomena determined by the mechanisms of associative memory finds support in the results of experiments on higher animals. Extirpation of the cerebral hemispheres causes complete loss of associative memory. After this operation, nothing remains that could possibly be interpreted by the metaphysicians as a phenomenon of consciousness.

If the cerebral hemispheres of a *Rana esculenta* or *temporaria* be extirpated, the frog seems on the whole to be unchanged. This has been proved beyond question by Schrader (1). Such a frog catches flies, buries itself in the mud when the cold season comes, and changes its habitation from the land to the water, like a normal frog. None of these processes, however, are functions of associative memory; they depend upon inherited structures. The frog either has no associative memory or it is so insignificant that it does not in any way affect the behaviour of the frog. This explains the fact that the loss of the cerebral hemispheres, which produces so great a change in the personality of a higher animal, has much less effect on a frog. In the shark, nothing in the habits or reactions of the normal animal shows the existence of associative memory. Most of its reactions are inherited and composed of segmental reflexes. We find, correspondingly, that it shows very little change after the extirpation of the cerebral hemispheres, for in spite of their loss the segmental reflexes are preserved.

It would be a mistake to assume that the loss of the cerebral hemispheres in no way affects the animal. Its loss has a certain effect upon the segmental reflexes. Nereis has no associative memory, yet it shows a certain lack of inhibition after the loss of the supra-œsophageal ganglion (see Chapter VI.). Something similar is noticeable in lower Vertebrates whose cerebral hemispheres are removed. For instance, in adders all segmental reflexes are preserved after loss of the cerebral hemispheres. Schrader found, however, that such animals no longer show any " fear "—it was not possible to frighten them although all the opticus-reflexes still functioned (2). From this we must conclude that the effects of those stimuli which extend from the opticus-segment into the central nervous system are different, so long as the cerebral hemispheres exist, from what they are when the hemispheres have been extirpated. Something of this kind also shows itself in the frog. Goltz has found that the frog without cerebral hemispheres is better suited for demonstrating reflexes than the frog with cerebral hemispheres. If the skin on the back of a normal frog is touched, it may or may not croak. Goltz showed that this croaking reflex never fails in a frog whose cerebral hemispheres have been excised (3). In the normal frog, however, touching the skin of the back produces, in addition, another reflex : it shows a tendency to leap away. The normal frog as well as the frog without cerebral hemispheres is a reflex animal—that is, its reactions are chiefly segmental reflexes. But there is this difference between the two : In the animal with cerebral hemispheres the same stimulus can produce more than a single reflex, and this fact adds to the greater complication and capriciousness of the reactions of the animal. On the other hand, the cerebral hemispheres can also restrict the play of the segmental reflexes. The clasping reflex of the male frog in the act of copulation is a segmental reflex of the arm-segments during the period of heat. It seems that sexual substances determine this reflex, since it cannot be shown to exist in animals that are castrated before the period of heat. Now male frogs that have lost the cerebral hemispheres are much more indifferent in the choice of the object they clasp during the period of heat than animals with cerebral hemispheres.

2. In birds the conditions are different from those which exist in frogs and sharks. We are indebted to Schrader for an exact and, in many respects, classic investigation of the effect of the extirpation of the

cerebral hemispheres on birds (4). The work of this investigator, Goltz's article on the dog without cerebral hemispheres, and Goltz's and Ewald's article on the dog with shortened spinal cord are among the best on the physiology of the central nervous system. Until their work appeared, it was a dogma (and is still in many text-books) that animals which have lost the cerebral hemispheres can no longer move spontaneously. Flourens is responsible for the statement. Schrader first disproved it in regard to the frog and then succeeded in disproving it in the case of birds. " None of the animals under observation [pigeons] showed a sleep-like condition longer than three to four days [after excision of the cerebral hemispheres]. According to Rolando and Flourens, animals which have undergone this operation, except when certain stimuli are applied to the skin, remain absolutely quiet. At first, this is true. The pigeons remain standing, where they are placed, with ruffled feathers, the head drawn in, the eyes closed, and often on one leg. Occasionally they shake themselves, clean their feathers with their beak, stretch sleepily, and in the act of defæcation take a few steps. If left undisturbed, nothing else is to be observed. When thrown up into the air, they fly down diagonally, strike obstacles, and fall rather than alight on the floor, where they at once sink back into their stupor again. If the skin is stimulated, they take a few steps, but in so doing are liable to run into obstacles " (Schrader, *loc. cit.*).

The difference between Flourens's and Schrader's observations lies in the fact that Flourens considered this condition permanent, while Schrader showed that it lasts only a few days or until the " shock-effect " of the operation has passed off. The objection might be raised that Schrader did not entirely remove the hemispheres, but this was not the case. Schrader's experiments are masterpieces in regard to the perfection of the mode of operation. The contradiction in the statements of the two authors is due to the fact, as it so often is in brain-physiology, that the minor effects of the operation in one case were strong, in the other slight, or that one author based his opinion upon the most severe disturbances, the other upon the slightest disturbances. The latter is the only reliable method in physiology of the brain, because in addition to the disturbances caused by the loss of part of the brain, the shock-effects on the rest of the central nervous system also appear in the mosaic of symptoms. Schrader's experiments are models in regard to technique, but this cannot be said of Flourens's experiment, to which fact the excellent investigator Magendie vainly called attention.

In Schrader's experiments, a few days after the operation, *spontaneity not only returns, but is even increased.* The animal *wanders about in the room untiringly the greater part of the day.* It is not blind, for its movements are determined by visual impressions. Like the frog without cerebral hemispheres, it turns out to avoid obstacles. " Dusty window-glass, transparent bell-jars placed in their way were avoided just as much as chairs and table legs, or boards of different colours." It is evident that optic space-perception still continues, even when the cerebral hemispheres (and with them the associative memory) have disappeared entirely. If such a pigeon is placed in an uncomfortable position, it flies to another place with perfectly coördinated movements. Schrader gives the following description: "We place our pigeon on the cloth-covered stopper of a large bottle. The stopper is large enough to support the animal on both feet, and is placed in the middle of a large, empty room, so that the pigeon is one to two metres above the floor. For some minutes the pigeon sits with its head drawn in, its feathers ruffled, in a condition of sleep or inhibition; then it shakes itself and begins to turn around and look about; finally it stoops and with an exertion looks down on the floor as if it wished to measure the height. It makes preparations to fly down, stops again, however, turns about once more, and again directs its attention to the floor. The duration of this play varies, but at last it flies down in a slight curve and alights easily on the floor. If a cross-bar is placed at the same height, one or two metres from the bottle, the pigeon flies determinedly to the bar and seats itself there. If a chair be used instead of a bar, the pigeon is seated on the arm" (4). These experiments show that these pigeons are able to measure distance by visual impressions also.

Schrader's observation is also of importance for the

solving of the problem as to whether sensations of space are purely a matter of memory, as Helmholtz, among others, assumes, or whether they are determined by inherited structural conditions, as Hering, for instance, maintains. The question is of great importance for the further investigation of the mechanics of the brain, and for this reason we mention it in passing. It has been assumed that space-sensations are acquired because the new-born infant does not immediately show signs of orientation in space. The fact is overlooked that the new-born infant comes into the world incomplete—that is to say, certain structures become complete during the first year or even later. The same erroneous conclusion was drawn in regard to walking. The child was supposed to " learn " to walk. The fact that the chick can walk when it comes out of the egg would have sufficed to prevent this error on the part of the empiricists, if physiologists had earlier appreciated the importance of comparative physiology. The difference between the chick and the human suckling consists in the fact that the structural development of the former is more complete at the moment of hatching than the structural development of the latter at the time of its birth. The child can begin to walk only when the nerves, muscles, etc., have reached the required degree of development. The same is true of visual space-perception. The newly hatched chick has visual perception ; that is, it picks at points that differ from their environment in colour and intensity of light.

It does not learn this reaction any more than a plant learns its heliotropic reactions, and it is no more necessary for the suckling than for the chick to learn space-reactions. They come " of themselves " as soon as the embryonic development of the suckling has advanced far enough. This conception, to which comparative physiology forces us, is further supported most effectually by Schrader's observation (and by those of earlier authors, for instance, Longet) that visual space-perception in birds continues after the cerebral hemispheres have been removed. The possibility that this holds good for birds and not for mammals is refuted by a statement of Christiani in regard to rabbits. The fact, however, that space-reactions can be modified by the memory, that we can " learn " to shave before a mirror, for instance, or can " learn " to grasp things in spite of prismatic glasses, does not contradict this conception any more than the acquired accomplishments of the dancer contradict the fact that normal walking is not a matter of memory. The fact that coördinated progressive movements on the turn-table occur in the direction of the plane of the rotation, and those produced by a galvanic current occur in the direction of the curves of the current, also speaks for this nativistic conception.

From this digression we will now return to Schrader's experiments. The pigeon described above as wandering about the room all day, sleeps at night. Sleep has nothing to do with consciousness and memory, for it occurs in plants. It is not surprising then that the animal without cerebral hemispheres shows the difference between sleeping and waking.

The great difference between the normal male pigeon and the pigeon that has lost its cerebral hemispheres is shown forcibly by the following facts: During the period of heat the male pigeon courts the female with cooing, but if a female pigeon is placed before the cooing male whose hemispheres have been removed, it remains unheeded. This entire lack of memory is the chief point in which the animal without cerebrum differs from the normal animal. "For the former everything is only a mass in space, it moves aside for every pigeon or attempts to climb over it, just as it would in the case of a stone. All authors agree in the statement that to these animals all objects are alike. They have no enemies and no friends. They live like hermits no matter in how large a company they find themselves. The languishing coo of the male makes as little impression upon the female deprived of its cerebrum as the rattling of peas or the whistle which formerly made it hasten to its feeding place. Neither does the female show interest in its young. The young ones that have just learned to fly pursue the mother, crying unceasingly for food, but they might as well beg food of a stone" (4).

Taking all the reactions of the pigeon without cerebral hemispheres together, it seems to me that the conclusion may be drawn that loss of the cerebral hemispheres causes the loss of the associative memory. Inherited reactions remain after the loss of the cerebrum, but that which is acquired by the activity of memory during the life of the individual is lost forever.

In order to emphasise this loss of memory after extirpation of the hemispheres, we will quote the following observation made by Schrader on a falcon. The falcon, as everyone knows, is a good hunter. Schrader placed some mice, and a falcon from which the hemispheres had been removed in the same cage. Every time that a mouse moved the falcon jumped on it and caught it in its claws, if the movement occurred within its field of vision. The normal falcon in such cases devours the mouse, but for the falcon without cerebral hemispheres the matter was at an end when the mouse was caught. The activity of the associative memory was lacking and the mouse was forgotten as soon as it ceased to move. When the falcon moved, the mouse escaped, but if the mouse moved again the process was repeated. Any inanimate object that moved would, of course, be caught in the same way. The falcon and mice remained together until one day the mouse devoured the back of the living falcon. Deprived of its memory the falcon was entirely defenceless (2).

One disturbance takes place in animals that have lost the cerebrum which does not belong in the same class with disturbances of memory, namely, the inability to take food unassisted. In frogs and, according to Steiner's observations, also in fishes (5), the ability to take food independently continues to exist after excision of the cerebral hemispheres. Birds without cerebral hemispheres starve unless they are fed. Schrader came to the conclusion that this is due to a disturbance of the motor innervation, for they are unable to swallow a pea placed in the front part of the beak ; to be swallowed it must be placed well back toward the throat. From the results of these experiments on frogs, I believe that we might go one step farther than Schrader and conclude that, in this case, the tension is decreased in certain groups of muscles which are necessary for taking food independently. We shall again meet with such a decrease in the tension of certain muscles after lesion of the cerebral hemispheres. This decrease in tension is, however, a secondary effect of the operation on the remaining segmental tracts of the central nervous system, and is not determined by loss of the cerebrum. It is very probable too that if Schrader's experiments are continued birds may be found in which disturbances in eating will not occur.

3. The bold attempt to remove both hemispheres entirely from a full-grown dog and then to keep it alive not only for months but for years has been attempted and carried on successfully by Goltz (6). The results of his experiments in a few words are as follows : In such a dog all those reactions in which the associative memory plays a rôle are lacking permanently, while the simple reactions that only depend on inherited conditions remain just as in pigeons and in other animals.

The dog without cerebral hemispheres sleeps and

wakes. It moves spontaneously—that is, without visible external stimulus. The only abnormal feature in the progressive movements of the dog without cerebral hemispheres was its extreme restlessness. When not asleep it moved about in the cage unceasingly, and this perhaps accounts for the fact that such animals show a tendency to lose flesh. The postures peculiar to dogs in urinating and defæcation were still assumed by these dogs. The reactions to sensory stimuli were normal in so far as no associative memory was necessary. Meat and milk were devoured greedily, but if made bitter with quinine they were ejected. The dog growled and snapped if its paw was pinched. If its foot was placed in cold water it was removed at once. If one paw was injured the dog was still able to go on three legs. If it was asleep it could be waked by blowing a horn in the next room. If in a dark room it closed its eyes when a strong light was suddenly allowed to strike it. It seemed more wide-awake and restless when it was hungry and more quiet after it had been fed. In regard to eating, the dog without cerebral hemispheres was more normal than Schrader's doves. To make the dog eat, it was only necessary to hold the plate up to its nose, so that the nose came in contact with the meat. The facts that motor disturbances exist and that such dogs do not turn out for obstacles, behaving in this regard like blind dogs, may be regarded as shock-effects on the brachial and optic segments, produced by the operation. The dog could still bark and howl.

But everything requiring associative memory was gone. The dog was not able to seek its food. It recognised neither its master nor its playmates. It could hear but could not discriminate between scolding and petting. It was impossible for it to get itself out of any uncomfortable situation. The period of heat was no longer noticeable. The effects are similar to those upon pigeons, with the difference that the secondary effects of the operation on the remaining parts of the central nervous system are greater in dogs. The reasons for this may be purely technical or anatomical, or may be due to a greater sensitiveness of the central nervous system in dogs. We may mention in this connection that hemorrhages in the human cerebral hemispheres are often accompanied by a complete paralysis of the extremities, while this is never the case in dogs.

The fact that in animals which normally possess no memory, loss of the hemispheres occasions little disturbance, and the fact that in animals possessing memory, the latter disappears upon destruction of the hemispheres, prove that the hemispheres are an essential organ for the phenomena of associative memory.

4. Pflüger expressed the opinion many years ago that an animal that has lost its brain still possesses consciousness (7). He drew this conclusion from the reactions of decapitated animals. If the tail of a decapitated eel be rubbed gently on one side the tail presses itself against the finger, but if touched with a burning match it is turned away. From these and

similar observations, which are doubtless correct, Pflüger concluded that the spinal cord possesses consciousness. Pflüger's statements gave rise to a lively discussion. His opponents could not refute his conclusions entirely, but they advanced arguments to show that the spinal cord does not possess consciousness. Goltz's ingenious experiments deserve special mention in this connection (3). They show that the decapitated frog is not able to rescue itself from an unpleasant situation. A blinded but otherwise normal frog and a frog without cerebral hemispheres were placed together in a trough filled with water and the water heated gradually. When the temperature of the water rose, the blinded frog became restless, jumped about, and attempted to escape from the trough. The frog without cerebral hemispheres, on the other hand, remained quiet and the heat rigor overcame it in the attitude it assumed when put into the trough. This of course speaks against the presence of consciousness in the spinal cord. But since this did not directly prove the erroneousness of Pflüger's conclusions, opinions remained divided. I believe we are now in a position to prove that Pflüger's observations not only allow but demand an entirely different explanation, and that it is wrong to make them a criterion for the existence of consciousness. The experiment with the tail of the eel is a case of tropism. The eel is positively stereotropic. It is forced to bring every part of its body as far as possible in contact with solid bodies, like Nereis, many insects, the stolons of Hydroids, and the roots of many plants. It lives chiefly in cracks. This is no more a process of consciousness than the boring of a root in the sand. It exists in every segment of the eel, and if touched on one side with the finger positively stereotropic curvations toward the finger ensue. The stimulus of rubbing increases the tension of the muscles on the stimulated side. But while it is positively stereotropic it is not positively thermotropic. If a burning object is applied it produces a relaxation of those muscles which move the body toward the stimulated side.[1] The body is thus moved toward the opposite side. In this case too consciousness plays no more part than it does in the tropic reactions of a plant. The whole discussion of the " spinal-cord-soul " was needless, and might have been avoided if Pflüger had realised that those phenomena which the metaphysician calls consciousness are a function of the mechanism of associative memory. In that case the question would have been :— Does the decapitated animal still possess associative memory, or are its reactions all due to inherited structures and irritabilities? With the aid of comparative physiology it would have been found that all the reactions of such an animal may occur in forms which possess no associative memory. The mechanisms which allow an associative memory in Vertebrates seem to be located in the cerebral hemispheres. In

---

[1] If Pflüger had made his experiments on decapitated snakes he would have obtained different results. Exner mentions that such animals press their body against a fiery coal just as well as against the finger (13).

Invertebrates they will probably be found in the supraœsophageal ganglion.

5. The spinal-cord-soul is not the only instance in which biologists have been led astray by their blind acceptance of metaphysical notions. A second and perhaps more general instance is the assumption that consciousness exists in every animal and is present to a certain degree even in the egg. Many authors object to the idea that a thing like consciousness or the soul should get into the body suddenly at a certain stage of development. What they consider true for the ontogenetic development they also assume for the phylogenetic development, and they are led to believe that each animal possesses consciousness. All these speculations collapse as soon as we free ourselves from the influence of metaphysics, and realise that the term consciousness or soul is applied by metaphysicians to phenomena of associative memory, and that the latter depends upon a physical mechanism which must be just as definite as, for example, the dioptrical apparatus of our eye. I do not think that anybody maintains that every animal must have an apparatus which unites the rays of light emanating from a luminous point to an image point on the surface of its body, simply because *certain* animals have such an apparatus. Moreover, I do not believe that even our biological metaphysicians assume that this dioptrical apparatus exists already in the human egg, and that the latter is already capable of visual space-perception, because it would be too awkward to as-

sume that visual space-perception should begin at a definite period of embryonic or post-embryonic development. And yet the matter is in no way different for psychic phenomena, if we realise that what we call psychic is only a metaphysical term for functions of associative memory. Just as our dioptrical apparatus can only begin to function after the eye has reached a certain stage of development, the mechanism of associative memory can only begin to function after the brain has reached a certain stage of development. And just as only *certain* animals are provided with apparatus for visual space-perception, only *certain* animals are provided with the mechanism necessary for associative memory.[1] I think it is time for us to realise that some of the phenomena of embryonic development are not continuous processes but decidedly discontinuous. This is, of course, less obvious if we limit our study of the organism to methods of staining and sectioning, but it becomes very striking if we add some physiological methods. A pure $\frac{5}{8}$ n NaCl solution is extremely poisonous to the eggs of Fundulus during the first twelve hours. After that it is decidedly less harmful. There is then a discontinuity in the physical or chemical conditions of that embryo at about twelve hours after fertilisation. Another discontinuity is connected with the beginning of circulation. Before circulation begins a $\frac{5}{8}$ n KCl solution is no more harmful to the embryo of Fundulus

---

[1] These considerations dispose also of the conception of consciousness in plants or of the barbarous notion of consciousness in molecules and atoms.

than a $\frac{5}{8}$ n NaCl solution. As soon as the heart begins to beat, the KCl becomes much more poisonous than the NaCl solution. A similar discontinuity is noticed if we try the effects of lack of oxygen. As soon as the circulation begins, the Fundulus embryo becomes quite suddenly much more sensitive to a lack of oxygen. The functional changes in the embryo itself are sudden and not gradual or continuous. The heart-beat, for example, starts at a certain time, suddenly, after a certain stage of development has been reached.

The idea of a steady, continuous development is inconsistent with the general physical qualities of protoplasm or colloidal material. The colloidal substances in our protoplasm possess critical points. If we increase the pressure of a gas below a certain temperature, at a certain critical point the gas becomes liquid. The colloids change their state very easily, and a number of conditions — temperature, ions, enzymes—are able to bring about a change in their state. Such material lends itself very readily to a discontinuous series of changes, while a gradual steady development, such as most Darwinians assume, is practically excluded.

We, of course, concede that the associative memory shows different degrees of development or perfection in different animals. These different degrees are mainly differences in capacity and resonance. By difference in capacity I mean a difference in the number of associations of which the brain is capable.

By difference in the resonance I mean the ease with which associations are produced. It is necessary, for example, in the case of a great complex of sensations, that the images of memory which correspond to certain constituents of that complex are easily reproduced, and in the case of a very elementary sensation greater images of memory, which contain that elementary sensation as a constituent, should be reproduced. The quality of resonance is perhaps the more important, as long as the capacity does not fall below the average. The intelligent man differs from the stupid man, among other things, in the ease with which by means of the associative memory he makes the analysis or synthesis of the complexes of sensation : that is, in the slow or stupid man only such images of memory are called up associatively as were connected before with the entire stimulating complex ; while in the quick thinker complexes of memory are also produced associatively which are connected with single elements of the stimulating complex.

6. After what has been said, it is clear that the absolute mass of the brain cannot be the principal factor in determining intelligence (10). In different races of dogs, for instance, the brain varies just as much as the weight of the body. Dogs of a small breed may, however, be more intelligent than dogs of a large breed. It also follows from this that the relation of mental activity to the metabolism of the central nervous system is totally different from that of muscular activity to the metabolism of the muscle. The

power-rate of activity of the muscles is proportional to their mass, and something similar may be true of the glands. The results obtained by weighing the brain of man have proved, conclusively, that the mass of the cerebrum, unless it falls below a certain minimum, in no way affects the degree of intelligence. The same facts prove that the number of ganglion-cells bears no direct relation to the degree of intelligence. The small dog has fewer ganglion-cells than the large dog, inasmuch as the size of the cells varies comparatively little in dogs of different size.

Speck, who has called attention to this difference between muscles and brain (8), has also made another important discovery, namely, that in case of lack of oxygen associative memory first disappears. He inhaled air deficient in oxygen from a gasometer, and counted during his experiments. As soon as the partial pressure of the oxygen of the air fell below 8 % of one atmosphere, he forgot to count very soon and then fainted, although the other functions of his body showed no change. Speck concludes from this that the cerebral hemispheres are most sensitive to a lack of oxygen. It is not absolutely necessary to conclude from this that the cerebral hemispheres have relatively the greatest metabolism of all the organs. It is possible that lack of oxygen affects the physical qualities of colloids in the brain in such a way as to make the functioning of the mechanisms of associative memory impossible. I have shown that lack of oxygen leads to a liquefaction of the cell-walls in certain forms, and it seems to be pretty generally true that the formation of solid cell-walls becomes impossible under such conditions (11). It is possible that in the case of lack of oxygen, physical changes in the state of certain constituents of the brain are prevented which are necessary for the activity of memory.

Some physiologists seem to be of the opinion that when the brain contains a good deal of blood the body has a special feeling of happiness. I recall a popular lecture by a prominent psychiatrist in which he maintains that when the cerebral hemispheres contain a great deal of blood the proprietor of this brain enjoys the absolute happiness (?) of an intoxication from champagne. This psychiatrist evidently imagines that the greater the supply of blood is, the better the brain is nourished, and that with the increasing nourishment of the brain the feeling of happiness increases. Among the food-substances which are offered to the brain in large quantities by the dilatation of the arteries oxygen takes the first place. It was formerly assumed that the oxygen-supply determined the metabolism, but we now know definitely that internal processes in the tissues determine the consumption of oxygen, probably processes of fermentation. If a certain quantity of oxygen is present in the brain, the superfluous oxygen has no effect. The same is probably true of all the other food-constituents. Under normal conditions the oxygen-supply in the brain is sufficient as long as the circulation is normal. It harmonises with these facts that mental activity does not influence the phenomena of oxidation, as Speck has proved by very careful experiments. But from this we must not conclude that the activity of the brain takes place without chemical changes, only that the chemical changes which are determined by mental activity are too slight to be recognised. The statement that dilatation of the blood-vessels of the brain produces a sensation of happiness is not based upon any fact that has been proved scientifically.

7. The amœboid changes in the ganglion-cells have been utilised to account for the phenomena of association. As far as normal processes of association are concerned, these amœboid changes cannot play any rôle, as they are much too slow. We notice migrations of the cones and the pigment in the retina, yet the idea that these protoplasmic motions play any rôle for space- or colour-perception has to be abandoned for the same reason.

Other authors hold that conditions of incomplete association, as in the case of dreams, or interruption of association, as in the case of deep sleep or narcotics, are due to a partial or complete disconnection of the ganglion-cells by a shortening of the processes. It does not seem to me that the observations which we thus far possess prove anything of that character (9, 12).

17

BIBLIOGRAPHY.

1. SCHRADER, MAX E. G. *Zur Physiologie des Froschhirns.* *Pflüger's Archiv*, Bd. xli., 1887.

2. SCHRADER. *Die Stellung des Grosshirns im Reflexmechanismus.* *Archiv für experiment. Pathologie und Pharmakologie*, Bd. xxix., 1892.

3. GOLTZ, F. *Beiträge zur Lehre von den Nervencentren des Frosches.* Berlin, 1868.

4. SCHRADER, MAX E. G. *Zur Physiologie des Vogelgehirns.* *Pflüger's Archiv*, Bd. xliv., 1889.

5. STEINER, J. *Die Functionen des Centralnervensystems und ihre Phylogenese.* II. Abth. : *Die Fische.* Braunschweig, 1885.

6. GOLTZ. F. *Der Hund ohne Grosshirn.* *Pflüger's Archiv*, Bd. li., 1892.

7. PFLÜGER, E. *Die sensorischen Functionen des Rückenmarks.* Berlin, 1853.

8. SPECK. *Physiologie des menschlichen Athmens.* Leipzig, 1892.

9. DUVAL, M. *Théorie histologique du sommeil.* *C. R. Soc. de Biol.*, 1895.

10. DONALDSON, H. H. *The Growth of the Brain.* London, 1895.

11. LOEB, J. *Untersuchungen über die physiologischen Wirkungen des Sauerstoffmangels.* *Pflüger's Archiv*, vol. lxii., 1895.

12. BAWDEN, H. H. *A Digest and a Criticism of the Data upon which is Based the Theory of Amœboid Movements of the Neuron.* *The Journal of Comparative Neurology*, vol. x., 1900.

13. EXNER, S. *Entwurf zu einer physiologischen Erklärung der psychischen Erscheinungen.* Leipzig and Wien, 1894, p. 85.

CHAPTER XVII

ANATOMICAL AND PSYCHIC LOCALISATION

1. It follows from the facts of the preceding chapter that the cerebral hemispheres are a necessary organ for the phenomena of associative memory. We are not quite justified in saying that they are the specific organ for this function. It may be possible, although not probable, that other parts of the brain are also required for this purpose. It is certain that the spinal cord is not needed for this function, for animals whose spinal cord is severed, or from whom the greater part of it has been removed, show no deficiency in the process of associative memory.

The cerebral hemispheres form an appendage of the segmental central nervous system. They are connected with at least some of the segmental ganglia by special nerve-fibres. As these different bundles of fibres enter the cortex at different places, it is obvious that if we stimulate the various spots of the surface of the cortex with electric currents of the smallest intensity necessary to produce a reaction, we must notice different effects. If, for instance, a current of minimal intensity be sent through the spot D (Fig.

39), where the fibres from and to the brachial segment of the cord of a dog enter the cortex, contractions of certain muscles of the fore-leg must follow. If we stimulate the region A (Fig. 39), which is connected with the sensory or motor ganglia of the eyes, motions of the latter must be produced. It is, moreover, evident that if we *injure* the spot D in the cortex we must get somewhat different after-effects from those produced when A is injured. In the former case we must expect motor disturbances in the use of the fore-leg, in the latter disturbances of vision.

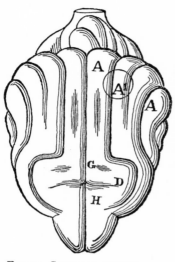

FIG. 39. CEREBRAL HEMISPHERES OF A DOG.

A, optical region; D, brachial region; G, region of the hind-leg. (After Munk.)

It is, of course, not to be expected that the distribution of segmental fibres on the cortex follows minutely the arrangement of the ganglia in the spinal cord. Displacements of elements occur in the cerebral hemispheres during the process of growth. This is indicated by the formation of folds formed on the surface. It is possible that not all the segmental ganglia send fibres directly to the hemispheres, and it is possible that certain ganglia are connected with the cortex at more than one spot or region. From the fact that the different bundles of fibres from the various segmental ganglia enter at different spots in the cortex, some authors have drawn the conclusion that there is not only an *anatomical localisation of fibres*, but also a *psychic localisation of functions*. They assume that the various psychic functions take place in different regions of the cortex. The occipital region, where the fibres from the segmental ganglia of the optic nerve enter, is considered by these authors as the seat of visual consciousness. At the spot D (where the brachial fibres enter or leave) the " consciousness of the fore-leg " is said to be localised. These assumptions are contradicted by the plain facts of associative memory. Simultaneous processes in different sense-organs are fused in our memory. The odour of a rose recalls its visual image. This could not be possible if the visual processes were confined to one region of the cerebral hemispheres ; they must spread to the olfactory region, and *vice versa*. The same can be said of other kinds of stimulation and of combinations of more than two stimuli. Moreover, we remember not only simultaneous sense-impressions, but we remember a whole series dependent upon successive stimuli of different character, if only the first constituent of such a series has been aroused. This indicates that even the after-effects of a stimulus must spread all over the cerebral hemispheres, so that they may fuse with the successive processes going on in the brain. It is thus obvious that the assumption of a localisation of psychic functions in the cortex is opposed to the elementary facts of associative memory or consciousness.

2. Experiments on the brain indicate that while there exists to a certain extent an anatomical localisation in the cortex, the assumption of a psychical localisation is contradicted by the facts. The occipital region of the cerebral hemispheres is said to be the seat of visual processes, the temporal lobes the seat of auditory processes. If the occipital regions are removed, only the visual processes are said to cease, while if the temporal regions are removed, only the auditory processes are said to disappear. We know that persons who were born blind and deaf have shown a normal or even a superior intellect (Laura Bridgman). If the theory of psychic localisation were correct, we should expect that an animal from whose hemispheres the occipital and temporal regions are removed would become blind and deaf, but would remain normal in other directions. But Goltz has shown that such an animal (dog) becomes hopelessly idiotic (2, V.). The processes of association even of the other senses are no longer normal. This agrees with the idea that in processes of association the cerebral hemispheres act as a whole, and not as a mosaic of a number of independent parts.

Goltz has proved that if we remove one whole hemisphere in a dog the personality of the animal or, in other words, the sum-total of its associations remains the same. The dog recognises its friends and all the other objects it has ever known, and it reacts in such a way as to indicate that its associative memory has not suffered through the operation. But if the anterior parts of both hemispheres be removed, the dog is no longer normal, but idiotic. It no longer reacts in the same way it did before, and it is obvious that its associative memory has suffered. The same is true if both posterior halves of the cerebral hemispheres be removed (2, V.).

If we ask at present what determines this difference, we are at a loss to give an answer. We might point out that the right and left hemispheres are practically symmetrical, while the anterior and posterior parts are not symmetrical. If the form or orientation of the elements be of importance, we might conceive of the possibility that in a brain with only one cerebral hemisphere all the processes could occur in approximately the same form, while in the brain with *both* posterior or *both* anterior halves of the hemispheres gone, the processes of association could not be repeated in the same, but in a mutilated form. Hence the idiocy which follows such operations. We might illustrate this by an analogous experience in the physiology of sound. Each vowel is determined by a sound of a certain pitch. If a singer sings in a pitch higher than that of the determinant, the vowel becomes indistinct. It is possible that in the brains of the above-mentioned dogs the associations are rendered impossible or difficult, because certain elemental processes are no longer possible.

3. In this connection I may mention that the bo-

servations of Goltz indicate a connection of the main regions of the cerebral hemispheres with certain regions in the medulla oblongata. A dog that has lost the anterior halves of both cerebral hemispheres has a tendency to run with its head bent down. A dog which has lost the posterior halves of both hemispheres shows the opposite tendency. It moves very little and its head is carried high in the air. Its anterior legs are stiff and often stretched forward. The difference in the position and progressive motions of these two animals seems to be somewhat similar to the difference in the attitude of an Amblystoma when stimulated by constant currents. The position of the dog in which the anterior halves of the cerebral hemispheres are removed resembles that of an Amblystoma in a descending current, while the attitude of the dog without the occipital halves of the hemispheres is like that of an Amblystoma in an ascending current. (See Chapter XI.) If in a dog one cerebral hemisphere be removed, while the other is intact, the dog makes circus-motions toward the injured side. There is an unmistakable analogy between these observations and the older experiments of Magendie and Flourens on the sectioning of the crura cerebelli.

While dogs after the loss of the anterior halves of the cerebral hemispheres often become irritable and ugly, dogs which lose the occipital halves of both hemispheres invariably become good-natured and harmless. This indicates a connection of the cerebral hemispheres with organs of the body for which with our present knowledge of anatomical localisation we cannot yet account.

4. Those who believe in a psychic localisation in the cerebral hemispheres base their claims chiefly on the effects of small lesions. If our point of view is correct, we should expect that small lesions either make no noticeable functional disturbance at all, or cause disturbances which are no more psychic than those following the cutting of a peripheral nerve. Hitzig and Fritsch were the first to destroy the cortex of the centre of the fore-leg (D, Fig. 39) in one of the hemispheres of a dog (1). When this centre was destroyed in the left hemisphere, the right leg showed the following disturbance : " In running, the animals did not use the right fore-paw to advantage. It was turned in or out too much and did not furnish a proper support. This never happened with the other paws. Movement did not fail entirely, but in the right leg the movement of adduction was somewhat weaker. In standing, the dorsal side of the paw was often used instead of the sole " (1). If the paw was placed in abnormal positions, no attention was paid to it by the dog. Hitzig and Fritsch draw the following conclusions from these observations : " The animals evidently had only an imperfect *consciousness* of the condition of this limb ; *they had lost the ability to form perfect ideas concerning it*." In the opinion of Hitzig we have to deal with a psychical disturbance, or, as we should say, a disturbance of associative memory. This disturbance of associative memory is, however, confined to such

processes as involve the right fore-leg. In our opinion, the phenomena observed by Hitzig are the outcome of a weakening of certain groups of muscles and a diminution of the sensibility in the right leg. Such disturbances could just as well be produced by a pressure upon certain peripheral nerve-fibres.

That Hitzig's psychological interpretation of his observation is wrong has been proved by Goltz. If Hitzig's idea were correct, we ought to assume that, if the centre of the right fore-leg were removed, a dog should no longer be able to use the right paw as a hand, where such a use is based upon the activity of associative memory. Goltz not only removed the centre but the entire left hemisphere of a dog that had been taught to dig its food out of a heap of pebbles. This dog showed all the disturbances of the right leg which Hitzig described. Yet it continued to dig its food (pieces of meat) out of the heap of pebbles with the right fore-paw. It preferred to use the left paw for this purpose. But when this was forbidden it used the right paw with success. This experiment proves that the conscious or psychical character of the motions of the fore-leg is not affected by the removal of its cortical centre. A close observation of the way the dog uses this paw shows that certain muscle-groups must have suffered by the operation, and a closer analysis of these purely muscular disturbances explains the anomalies which Hitzig had mistaken to be of a psychical character. Removal of the fore-leg centre causes a decrease in the tension of the extensors of the leg (and perhaps also of other groups of muscles). For this reason the leg slips easily and bends in the ankle-joint so that the animal sometimes steps on the back instead of the sole of the foot. It does not notice if the leg is placed in an abnormal position. This is partly due to the diminution in resistance caused by the weakening of certain muscles and partly due to a reduction in the sensibility of the skin. Goltz has proved that it requires a greater pressure on the skin of this leg to cause the dog to withdraw it than on any of the other legs. This explains also why the dog does not notice if the foot whose cortical centre has been removed is placed in cold water. There are, then, changes in the tension of certain muscles and a reduction in the sensibility of the skin which suffice to explain all the disturbances observed by Hitzig, but there is no loss of muscular "consciousness" as Hitzig assumes. To a certain extent, similar effects can be produced by dividing the posterior roots of the arm-nerves. It would hardly occur to anyone to maintain for this reason that the psychic centre of the arm-movements is localised in the posterior roots. Further proof that these disturbances described by Hitzig are due to a decrease in the tension of the extensors is furnished by the fact that in man, when an arm becomes paralysed after a local disease in the cerebral hemispheres, a contraction producing a flexed position of the arm takes place after a time. Not all the muscles of the arm are completely paralysed as a result of the disease in the hemispheres; but the tension of the extensors has decreased, and as a result the tension of the flexors alone determines the position of the arm.

In Goltz's experiment the centre of the right fore-leg alone had been removed. It has been said that the centre of the left fore-leg situated in the other hemisphere performed the psychic functions for both legs after the operation. I made an experiment to which this objection is not possible. A dog was taught to walk on its hind-legs when it wanted to be fed. Then the hind-leg centres were removed (G, Fig. 39) in both hemispheres. In spite of this loss the dog was still able to walk on its hind-legs. Whenever I offered it food or whenever it expected to be fed it rose voluntarily on its hind-feet. *The conscious actions or associations for the use of the hind-legs had not suffered*, but there was decidedly a muscular disturbance inasmuch as the dog was not able to stand so long on its hind-legs as it could before the operation. I showed this dog at the naturalists' meeting in Berlin in 1886. The day after the demonstration I showed the brain of the animal that had been killed in the meantime. The hind-leg centres had been removed completely.

It must, however, be explicitly stated that not every limited lesion in the motor centres leads to a disturbance. This is not only of importance from a theoretical but also from a practical point of view. A physician need not be surprised if a post-mortem examination shows a circumscribed lesion in the cortex which had not caused any clinical symptoms. It is obvious that certain organs are more easily disturbed by a lesion in the cortex than others. An operation in the centre of the fore-leg produces disturbances more easily than an operation in the centre of the hind-leg. There are certain parts of the body in which no disturbances can be produced by the extirpation of their so-called centres in the cortex. Nobody has thus far been able to produce a paresis or paralysis of the upper eyelid in a dog or to produce loss of sensibility in the cornea by an operation in the cortex. It must, moreover, not be overlooked that all the disturbances which follow small lesions of the cortex in dogs are only transitory.

5. Not only the motor but also the sensory disturbances which follow an operation in the cerebral hemispheres have been interpreted as psychic disturbances. We know that a lesion of the surface of the occipital lobes causes visual disturbances. Munk has interpreted these disturbances which follow a small lesion of one of the visual spheres as psychic (4). There is a small region (A_1 Fig. 39) in each of the occipital lobes the destruction of which, according to Munk, causes a psychic blindness in the opposite eye. By psychic blindness Munk means the fact that the dog does not recognise what it sees, although it is by no means blind. If the cortex be removed at the region A_1 in the left hemisphere, the dog shows psychic blindness in the right eye. Such a dog, for instance, is no longer afraid of a burning match or of the whip,

provided its left eye be closed. Munk assumes that the image of memory of the whip or the burning match had been deposited in the region A_1 and was lost with the loss of this place. It can be shown that Munk is as much mistaken concerning the psychic character of the visual disturbance following the destruction of a small region in the occipital lobes, as Hitzig was in regard to the psychic character of the motor disturbances following the destruction of a centre of the fore-leg. In the majority of cases the removal of the region A_1 in one hemisphere produces no visual disturbance. In the cases where a visual disturbance is produced it is only temporary. I noticed indeed that such dogs may no longer recognise objects in the opposite eye, but the reason for this is altogether different from that assumed by Munk.

It is known that in man the destruction of the visual sphere in one hemisphere causes the same disturbance as the destruction of the optic tract of the same side—namely, a hemianopia of the opposite half of the visual field. This disturbance is not psychic but purely physiological, inasmuch as it results in a loss of irritability on one side of each retina, but not in a loss in the processes of association. The same occurs in a dog whose visual sphere has been injured in one spot, with this difference, however, that the loss of irritability is not complete. Thus if the left occipital region be injured in a man, a hemianopia of the left sides of both retinæ follows, and the patient sees nothing in the right half of his visual field. If the same operation be performed in a dog, it causes not a complete hemianopia but a hemiamblyopia (5). The dog is not blind for the right half of its visual field, but has only a reduced power of vision. It behaves like an animal that pays less attention to that half of its visual field, or whose threshold for this half is reduced. If we stand before such a dog and hold two pieces of meat in front of it, simultaneously, one piece in each hand, the dog invariably chooses the piece at its left. It almost seems as though it did not see the piece at the right. Now we know that a moving object acts as a stronger optical stimulus than a stationary object. If the two pieces of meat are again held before the dog in the manner described above, only with the difference that the piece that is in the right half of the field of vision is moved, the dog jumps at the latter (6). This proves that in the dog the threshold of stimulation for optical stimuli has been raised in the right half of the field of vision. But how could Munk mistake the hemiamblyopia for a psychic disturbance? In a dog, the divergence of the optical axes is greater than in man. Hence the right half of the visual field is controlled more by the right eye than by the left. If we produce the hemiamblyopia or the hemianopia in a dog, the eye opposite the injured hemisphere is blind or injured for considerably more than one half of its retina. If the other eye of such a dog be closed, its field of vision is reduced to a very small area, and the dog does not recognise the objects, although it is not entirely blind. What Munk mistook for psychic blindness is, in reality, only hemiamblyopia or hemianopia (5, 6).

6. One of the main arguments which Munk used for his assumption of a psychic character of the visual disturbances caused by the effects of a unilateral lesion of a visual sphere was the fact that these disturbances disappear in about six weeks. On the basis of this fact he constructed the following hypothesis: The visual images of memory are deposited each in a single ganglion-cell or a group of cells in the region A_1 of the opposite hemisphere. If this region be removed, the dog loses all its images of memory. But new images of memory can be deposited in the surrounding parts A. This will be done after the loss of the region A_1 and the dog becomes normal again after six weeks. If this hypothesis of Munk were correct, visual disturbances of such a dog should not disappear if it were kept in the dark, where it would have no chance to acquire new visual images of memory. I made that experiment. In dogs which possessed only the right eye, the region A_1 in the left cerebral hemisphere was destroyed. In the majority of these dogs, the operation produced no effect. In a few, hemiamblyopia occurred. Of these several were put in an absolutely dark room for the following six weeks. As soon as they were taken out they were entirely normal. This proves that their recovery was not due to the acquisition of new visual images of memory, but to the fact that a purely physiological effect upon

the irritability of the optical apparatus caused by the operation wears off after a certain time.

We then come to the conclusion that the apparent psychic blindness which follows the destruction of the region A_1 in the opposite hemisphere is exclusively a hemianopia or hemiamblyopia. This disturbance is no psychic disturbance inasmuch as it can be produced by an injury to a peripheral nerve, the optic tract.

7. We must seek an explanation for the temporary character of the disturbance which follows small lesions. If the lesion covers a large area, the disturbance is more permanent. Goltz assumes that these transitory effects are shock-effects due to the operation. He was led to this assumption through his experiments on the spinal cord. If the spinal cord be cut in a dog, no segmental reflexes occur during the first days or weeks after the operation in the part of the animal below the cut. " Pressing on the hind-feet produces no reaction. In the male dog, erection of the penis cannot be aroused reflexly. The urine collects in the relaxed bladder. The anus gaps. In brief, the whole posterior part of the body seems unirritable. A few days later the apparently dead spinal cord may have recovered almost entirely. The posterior part of the animal then offers a large number of reflex phenomena. No one will assume that that piece of the spinal cord which is separated from the brain in so short a time acquires entirely new powers as a reflex organ ; we must assume that these

18

powers were only suppressed or inhibited temporarily by the lesion of the spinal cord." The same is true in regard to the vasomotors. Division of the spinal cord reduces the tonus of the blood-vessels of the posterior legs. After a time the blood-vessels recover and become normal again. Now if the sciatic nerve in the same animal be severed, a new temporary paralysis of the vasomotors follows. This proves that the vasomotor paralysis in the hind-legs that occurs after the division of the spinal cord is due to a shock-effect of the operation. What the nature of this shock-effect is we do not know. Perhaps v. Cyon's experiment throws light on this : v. Cyon showed, namely, that the tension of the muscles decreases after the division of the posterior root of their segment (3).

8. We conclude from all these observations on dogs that small lesions do not cause any disturbances in the processes of associative memory, and that Hitzig and Munk are wrong in interpreting the disturbances following the excision of a small piece of the cortex as psychic disturbances. In the majority of cases such slight lesions cause no disturbance, and where any is caused it is of such a character as could be produced by the lesion of a peripheral nerve. If we wish to produce psychic disturbances by a lesion of the brain, we must destroy extensive parts of *both* hemispheres. Operations in one hemisphere alone, and even the destruction of an entire hemisphere, have no such effect.

It has been claimed that the intellect is the function of special parts of the brain. Hitzig and others assumed that the frontal lobes of the cerebral hemispheres are the organs of attention. I have repeatedly removed both frontal lobes in dogs (6). It was impossible to notice the slightest difference in the mental functions of the dog. There is perhaps no operation which is so harmless for a dog as the removal of the frontal lobes. Flechsig thinks that it is not only the frontal lobe but the cortex of certain other regions which is responsible for mental activity, inasmuch as it is the seat of " centres of association." I have removed the cortex of Flechsig's " centres of association " in dogs without having noticed anything that justifies Flechsig's hypothesis. The assumption of " centres of association " is just as erroneous as the assumption of a centre of coördination in the heart. Association is, like coördination, a dynamical effect determined by the conductivity of the protoplasm. Associative processes occur everywhere in the hemispheres (and possibly in other parts of the brain), just as coördination occurs wherever the connection between two protoplasmic pieces is sufficient. It is just as anthropomorphic to invent special centres of association as it is to invent special centres of coördination.

BIBLIOGRAPHY.

1. HITZIG, E. *Untersuchungen über das Gehirn*, Berlin, 1874 ; and *Reichert's und Du Bois-Reymond's Archiv*, 1870.
2. GOLTZ, F. *Ueber die Verrichtungen des Grosshirns.*

I. *Abhandlung Pflüger's Archiv*, Bd. xiii., 1876.
II. " " " " xiv., 1877.
III. " " " " xx., 1879.
IV. " " " " xxvi., 1881.
V. " " " " xxxiv., 1884.

3. v. Cyon, E. *Gesammelte Physiologische Arbeiten*, p. 197 a. f. Berlin, 1888.

4. Munk, H. *Ueber die Functionen der Grosshirnrinde.* Berlin, 1881.

5. Loeb, J. *Die Sehstörungen nach Verletzungen der Grosshirnrinde.* *Pflüger's Archiv*, Bd. xxxiv., 1884.

6. Loeb, J. *Beiträge zur Physiologie des Grosshirns.* *Pflüger's Archiv*, Bd. xxxix., 1886.

CHAPTER XVIII

DISTURBANCES OF ASSOCIATIVE MEMORY

1. We have mentioned the hypothesis that each image of memory is localised in a special ganglion-cell or a group of ganglion-cells. As soon as a new image of memory arrives, it is, according to this hypothesis, deposited in one of the empty cells. Who deposits it and who finds out which cell is empty and which occupied is a question the originators of such hypotheses do not ask. This conception treats the image of memory as if it were something substantial, *i. e.,* something characterised by mass.[1] Munk has asserted the possibility of proving that in a dog the single visual images of memory are localised in isolated cells, or groups of cells, at the part A_1 (Fig. 39). He gives as proof two experiments, " in which extirpation of the part A_1 caused the loss of all but one of the visual images of memory. One single visual image

[1] This peculiar hybrid between metaphysics and anatomy owes its origin largely to Gall. Gall was an industrious worker in the anatomy of the brain and at the same time a huge fraud. The anatomy of the brain was not sufficiently sensational for him, so he enlivened things somewhat by grafting upon his anatomy the worst metaphysics he could possibly get hold of. The various nooks and corners of the brain became the seat of soul-powers of his invention. This artificial connection between metaphysics and brain-anatomy or histology has since become traditional.

of memory in each case was found to be preserved and unimpaired : in one case the image of the pail, out of which the dog was accustomed to drink, remained ; in the other, that of the motion of the hand, which before the operation had been the signal for the dog to give its paw." It was this statement of Munk that led me as a student to make experiments on the brain. I hoped that a road to an exact psychology had been opened. I began my experiments as a confirmed supporter of Munk. The more experiments I made the more it became apparent that many of Munk's statements were incorrect, especially his meagre statements concerning the supposed localisation of single images of memory. It is my opinion that these histological or corpuscular hypotheses of the images of memory must be supplanted by dynamical conceptions. The dynamics of the process of association is the true problem of brain-physiology. Even if the hypotheses of psychic localisation were not contradicted by all the facts, the pointing out of the centres would not be a solution of the dynamical problem. By merely showing a student the location of a power-plant, we do not explain to him the dynamics of electric motors.

I have mentioned above the possibility that processes of association will become abnormal if certain elemental constituents are mutilated or impossible. I selected as an example our ability to recognise a vowel. If the vowel is sung at a pitch which excludes its specific formative sound, it becomes indistinct. A study of patients afflicted with amnesia seems to support this analogy. It is not possible to use all the reports of such cases. I think that the majority of practitioners have neither the training nor the time to analyse them. I will confine myself to two cases from the Clinic of Professor Rieger in Würzburg, one of which was analysed by himself (1), and the other by his assistant, Dr. Wolff (2). In the first case the patient had suffered a concussion of the brain in a railroad accident. Among a number of other disturbances, his memory showed peculiar gaps. The patient was able to recognise only the numbers 1, 2, and 3. The corpuscular theory of the images of memory would assume that all numbers which the patient had originally possessed had been located each in a special cell, and that these cells had all perished with the exception of the cells which contained the first three numbers. This at once seems strange ,and becomes still stranger when taken in connection with the following observation. In every case it took the patient some time to find the word *one* when the figure 1 was held before him. The reaction-time for naming a 2 was considerably longer, and for naming a 3 was still longer. He was able to reckon with these three numbers, but when a 3 occurred he required more time than when a 1 or a 2 occurred. The determination of the reaction-time furnishes the explanation of the fact that all numbers beyond 3 were wanting. All of Rieger's experiments on this patient showed that if he did not succeed in finding the name of an object within a certain time (about eighteen seconds) it was impossible for him to do so at all. Now for finding the word *three* when he was shown the figure 3 he required almost eighteen seconds, and in fact he even failed occasionally to find it. The first three numbers are the ones that a child first learns, and are also those used most frequently during life. We know that the words we use least are the ones most liable to vanish from our memory (for instance, the vocabulary of a foreign language). It is possible that in the brain of the patient the processes were partly mutilated or rendered more difficult. The numbers used most frequently could cross the threshold ; those used less frequently could not. This conception is further confirmed by the fact that by touching the edges the patient was able to distinguish a ten- from a fifty-pfennig piece, although the numbers ten and fifty were otherwise gone, and as stamped on the coins were only hieroglyphics to him. The money-conception of the ten- and fifty-pfennig piece had formed more associations and clung more tenaciously to the memory of this man, who had to struggle for his existence, than the abstract conceptions ten and fifty, which had existed in his head only as a scholastic luxury. Hence any adequate idea of the nature of the disease of this man must be a dynamic one. In the injured brain of this patient certain processes were able to take place as before, except that they were less intense or incomplete. Those innervations forming constituents of relatively many or important associations were still possible, or occurred in a more normal form, while other innervations became impossible or were mutilated. In this case it would be just as erroneous to assume that the single conceptions or letters are all localised in single cells, and that the corresponding cells in the patient had perished, as it would be erroneous to conclude in a case of interference of sounds that the source of vibration was removed.[1]

2. The second case mentioned is still clearer (2). The disturbance of associative memory was also caused by an accident. When the patient was asked the colour of the leaves of a tree, he was unable to answer the question unless he was allowed to go to the window and look at a tree. In this case he answered correctly. As long as he could not see a tree it was impossible for him to tell the colour of a leaf. Pieces of green, red, and blue paper were put before him, and he was asked which the leaves looked like, but he was unable to tell. If asked whether the trees were blue, he answered that this was possible. Only when looking at a tree was he able to remember that the leaves were green. When asked how many legs a horse has, he went to the window and waited until a horse passed by. This enabled him to find the word *four*. Only in winter was he able to tell the colour of snow. In summer he admitted the possibility that

---

[1] Conditions similar to those that existed in this patient can be artificially produced by the dynamometer-experiments which will be described in the next chapter.

snow is black. He was once asked the colour of the blood. He opened a little pustule on his hand, and as soon as a drop of blood came out he gave the answer, red.

It is obvious from these facts that the patient understood every question and was sufficiently intelligent to secure those impressions which allowed him to answer the question. He could tell the colour of sugar if allowed to look at it, but this did not help him to tell whether or not sugar tastes bitter. In order to do so he had to put the sugar into his mouth. When a smooth piece of glass was shown to him he could not tell that it was smooth until he had touched it.

Two things are evident—first, the patient was not able to remember any perceptible quality of an object unless the object was under his immediate perception; and second, he remembered the various qualities only if the specific senses for these qualities were affected. In a normal being the word *sugar* or the sight of sugar suffices to produce the association of its sweet taste. In this patient only contact with the tongue suggested the word *sweet*, although he was intelligent enough to know how to arouse the correct association.

The names of a great many objects may be suggested to a normal person through any of several of the senses. For example, we find the word *violin* if we see the object as well as if we hear it played without seeing it. The patient in this case was a violin player, but it was necessary for him to see the instrument before he could name it. When a key was put into his pocket and he was allowed to touch it he could not say what it was. He could, however, find the word if he could see the key in the door. When his hand was put to his ear, he could not tell what he touched unless he looked at the doctor's ear. When the doctor covered his own ear, the patient was unable to find the word. It is obvious that in his case the visual perception was, on the whole, more effective than any other sensation. A sense-perception was necessary to call forth the association of concrete objects, and of the many possible sense-perceptions, which in normal cases might have brought about the word, the strongest alone in him sufficed. The word *umbrella* was only suggested when the umbrella was opened. From this we might imagine that a change in the machinery of association had taken place, which allowed only the processes having a maximal intensity or amplitude to arouse an associative process, the others remaining without any effect.

The process was the same in regard to abstract associations. The patient complained that his annuity was too small. He remonstrated against the doctor's insinuation that he had murdered his wife or that he was a scamp. But whether a beggar is a wealthy or a poor man, or whether God lives in hell or in heaven, were problems which he was not able to decide, although he was a believer.

There was another peculiarity in his mechanism of

association which is in line with the necessity for
sense-impressions for the remembrance of words.
Before he was able to pronounce a word he had to
go through the motion of writing it. When asked
the colour of the leaves, he had to go to the window
and look at a tree, and then he had to go through
the motion of writing the word *green* with his finger
before he could give the correct answer. When not
allowed to use his fingers for this purpose, he used his
toes, and when this was forbidden, he made the writing
motions in his mouth with his tongue. When all
three motions were forbidden, he was not able to find
the word.[1] He did not write phonetically, but ortho-
graphically. It would be absurd to think for a moment that in this case one single centre, or one single
tract between two centres, was injured. The whole
apparatus was equally affected. I believe that the
associative mechanism of the patient differed only
in degree from the associative mechanism of a
normal being. Wolff pointed out that for each act
of remembering there is one association more powerful than the rest. But for a normal being the weaker
associations are sufficient for the reproduction, while
in our patient only the strongest one sufficed. One
may ask how it happens that we so seldom hear of
such simple, clear cases as those published by Rieger
and Wolff. I believe the majority of physicians who
deal with such patients have neither the scientific

---

[1] It was not necessary for him to *see* what he wrote or to actually write ; it
was sufficient to go through the *motions* of writing.

training nor sufficient time to make an exhaustive analysis of the case. Wolff's patient had been in the hands of half a dozen specialists, and they discovered only the peculiar writing motions that the patient used. This of course led them to false conclusions. If the analysis in such a case is incomplete, the results must be misleading.

3. It is worth while to compare the mental condition of these patients with that of lower animals. The two patients mentioned above forgot immediately what was said to them. If the correct association did not occur to them after a short time, the question had to be repeated. There was, however, one exception. Objects or occurrences which were intimately connected with their instincts they remembered—for instance, money matters. We can imagine that conditions may be similar in lower animals—*e. g.*, wasps, which either forget easily or only seem to remember certain things which are intimately connected with their instincts—*e. g.*, the location of the nest.

A qualitative difference has been supposed to exist between the associative memory of man and that of animals. These patients may help us to arrive at a decision in regard to this question. When the patient was asked the colour of blood, the question aroused associations which caused him to provide the visual impression of blood. If we compare with this the fact that a wasp is no longer able to find its nest when the latter is covered with a small blossom, we might imagine that there is a *qualitative* difference between the associative memory of the wasp and of man. It might be argued that man possessed the power of creating new associations, *i. e.*, the ability of substituting or changing the existing conditions, in order to make a new process of association possible. But this ability is not entirely lacking in animals. When in Thorndike's experiment a cat goes voluntarily into a certain cage and waits there to be offered a fish, we have to deal with the same apparent ability of creating new associations. On the other hand, the superiority of man in this direction can be accounted for by the fact that his capacity for forming and retaining new associations is very much greater than that of animals.

The question, What is the colour of blood? produces not only *one* association — the word *red* — but a number of other associations, for instance, the association of a wound and the association of the production of a wound. If at that time the sense-impression of a pustule occurs, the association arises that the opening of the pustule causes the appearance of blood. All experiments point to the fact that this overwhelming abundance of associations which even a disabled human brain can form is lacking in animals. One impression may arouse only a very limited number of associations. This is evident from Thorndike's experiments on dogs and cats (3), and from Whitman's observations on pigeons (4). This small capacity for associations makes the reactions of animals appear machine-like and less intelligent. I think that the greater capacity of the human brain for associations and the greater celerity with which these associations are formed and retained are sufficient to explain why mankind has been able to control nature, while animals remain at its mercy.

In a pamphlet on *Instinct and Intelligence*, Father E. Wasmann, S.J., a well-known entomologist, has raised the question as to whether or not animals possess intelligence (5). The answer to such questions varies with the definition of the word *intelligence*, and hence such discussions result in a discussion of words and definitions. Such scholastic discussions are very serviceable for the defence of a dogma or an opinion. Wasmann's pamphlet belongs in this category. But we cannot overlook the fact that the steady progress of science dates from the day when Galileo freed science from the yoke of this sterile scholastic method. The aim of modern biology is no longer word-discussions, but the control of life-phenomena. Accordingly we do not raise and discuss the question as to whether or not animals possess intelligence, but we consider it our aim to work out the dynamics of the processes of association, and find out the physical or chemical conditions which determine the variation in the capacity of memory in the various organisms.

BIBLIOGRAPHY.

1. RIEGER, K. *Beschreibung einer Intelligenzstörung in Folge einer Hirnverletzung*, etc. *Verhandl. der Würzburger physikalisch medicinischen Gesellschaft*, Bd. xxii. and xxiii., 1889 and 1890.

2. WOLFF, GUSTAV. *Ueber krankhafte Dissoziation der Vorstellungen.* *Zeitschrift für Psychologie und Physiologie der Sinnesorgane*, Bd. xv., 1897.

3. THORNDIKE, E. L. *Animal Intelligence.* *The Psychological Review*, vol. ii., 1898.

4. WHITMAN, C. O. *Animal Behaviour.* Biological Lectures Delivered at Wood's Holl, 1898. Boston, Ginn & Co.

5. WASMANN, E. *Instinct und Intelligenz im Thierreich.* Freiburg, 1897.

CHAPTER XIX

ON SOME STARTING-POINTS FOR A FUTURE ANALYSIS OF THE MECHANICS OF ASSOCIATIVE MEMORY

1. The facts have thus far shown that the reflexes are determined chiefly by the structure of the sense-organs, or of the surface of the body, and the arrangement of the muscles. The central nervous system participates in these functions only as a conductor. The true problem with which the physiology of the reflexes is concerned is the mechanics of protoplasmic conductivity. This problem is no longer a biological problem but a problem of physical chemistry.

The only specific function of the brain, or certain parts of it, which we have been able to find is the activity of associative memory. There is at present a tendency to consider the anatomical and histological investigation of the brain as the most promising line for the analysis of these functions. It seems to me that we can no more expect to unravel the mechanism of associative memory by histological or morphological methods than we can expect to unravel the dynamics of electrical phenomena by a microscopic study of cross-sections through a telegraph wire or by counting and locating the telephone connections in a big city.

If we are anxious to develop a dynamics of the various life-phenomena, we must remember that the colloidal substances are the machines which produce the life-phenomena. But the physics of these substances is still a science of the future. The new methods and conceptions created by physical chemistry give us the hope that a physics of the colloidal substances may be looked for in the near future. At present we can only consider data of secondary importance for the mechanics of associative memory. The first group of these data is furnished by the study of the functions of the sense-organs.

Helmholtz emphasised the fact that our senses only furnish us symbols of the external world. Every physical process that affects a sense-organ produces changes in the organ. These changes are determined by the peripheral structure or by the specific " energy " of the sense-organs, as physiologists since Johannes Müller call it. Whether a blow, an electric current, or ether-vibrations of about 0.0008–0.0004 mm. wave-length stimulate the retina, the sensation is always a specific one, namely, light, while a blow or an electric current produces sensations of sound in the ear. This so-called law of the specific energy of the sense-organs is not peculiar to the sense-organs ; it applies, as was emphasised by Sachs, to all living matter ; it even holds good for machines. It is in reality only another expression for the fact that the eye, the ear,

and every living organ are able to convert energy in
but one definite form — that is, that they are special
machines. The determination of the way in which
this transformation of energy occurs in the various
organs would be the explanation of the specific energy
of the various senses.

Physiology gives us no answer to the latter question. The idea of specific energy has always been
regarded as the terminus for the investigation of the
sense-organs. All the more credit is due Mach and
Hering for first having advanced beyond that limit
with their chemical theory of colour-sensations. Mach
has recently expressed the opinion that chemical
conditions lie at the foundation of sensations in
general (1).

For the eye we may consider it as probable that
light produces chemical effects. Various substances
are formed and decomposed in the retina, and the
chemical processes of the formation and decomposition of these substances determine the light- and
colour-sensations. The ether-vibrations of certain
wave-lengths influence these decompositions in a definite manner. The electro-magnetic theory of light
will probably in this case lead to further discoveries.
Effects similar to those produced by light are also
brought about by the electric current. The current
itself can pass through the retina only by means of
electrolysis, and it may be that the increase in the
concentration of ions (wherever their progress is
blocked) brings about the light- and colour-sensations

caused by the current. It is not impossible that the so-called visual substances—that is, the photo-sensitive substances—are electrolytes. We can thus understand how the electric current produces sensations of light and colour in the eye. But it is more difficult to account for the fact that pressure or a blow on the eyeball produces the sensation of a flash. Carey Lea has found that on photographic plates pressure produces changes of the same character as weak light.

The specific energy of the eye would accordingly amount to nothing more than the fact that an increase in the concentration of ions or certain other chemical substances in the retina causes the sensation of light and colour, no matter whether the changes are caused by vibrations of the ether, by the electric current, or by a blow on the eye. The stimuli which are transmitted to the brain from the eye will hence show exactly the variety and peculiarities which correspond to the variety and peculiarities of the chemical processes in the retina.

The same holds good for the stimuli which are transmitted to the brain from the organs of taste and from the nose. The chemical nature of the causes that produce the sensations of smell and taste is so apparent as to require no proof.

We find greater difficulty in dealing with the sense-organs of the skin. Yet it is conceivable that a chemical basis may also exist for the activity of these senses. This idea finds support in a train of thought, by which I attempted to explain the peculiar influence of gravity on the orientation of animals and plants and their formation of organs (2). In these cases, a change in the orientation of the organs produces a change in the chemical condition. If the chemical processes in these instances consist in fermentative processes, the amount of the chemical change in the unit of time must be a function of the number of the ferment-molecules and of the fermentable molecules that come in contact. If we assume that both are present in different morphological constituents of the living cells, that the ferment, for instance, is present in the nucleus, the fermentable substance in the protoplasm of the cell, it is apparent that a change in the position of the cell or a pressure upon it will bring new molecules of the protoplasm in contact with the nucleus. In this way the metabolic activity may be increased. Such changes in the peripheral nerve-endings of the skin might result in innervations and reflexes. But this is all so vague that it only indicates the possibility of the chemical character of the process. It seems forced, if not altogether impossible, to apply this theory to the cochlea of the ear. We could imagine that the vibrations of sound produce corresponding vibrations in the endings of the auditory nerve, by which new molecules are brought into contact with each other. But I cannot see how this assumption could account for the different pitches or the phenomena of consonance. While a chemical theory is possible or probable for certain sensations, *e. g.*, light, taste, and smell, it is very doubtful whether such a theory can be applied to the other sense-organs. But it is certain that if we wish to make any progress in this direction we must follow the lead of Mach and Hering, and must cease to consider the so-called law of the specific energy of the sense-organs as the terminus of our investigation of the processes of sensation.

2. If we wish to find out the dynamics of association we must study the effects which simultaneous processes have upon each other. Let us consider periodic and aperiodic processes.

If we turn a wheel with one hand without thinking of the manner or velocity of the rotation, and at the same time repeat a poem to ourselves without moving the lips, the number of the revolutions shows a simple numerical relation to the number of the arses of the verses. In German, where the arsis is pronounced with greater emphasis than the thesis, the number of the rotations of the wheel generally equals the number of the arses. Brücke first called attention to this relation. Thirteen years ago I made a large number of experiments (not published) concerning this subject that yielded the same result. But I found, further, that if one intentionally turns the wheel rapidly and recites slowly, the number of rotations is a simple multiple of the arses. Two, three, or even more revolutions are made in the interval of one arsis. If one recites very rapidly and turns the wheel very slowly, the number of the arses becomes a simple multiple of the number of revolutions. In the latter case, the number of revolutions is often the same as the number of verses. If we assume that in thinking the poem the respiratory innervations which follow the rhythm can be represented as harmonic curves, and that the same holds good for the innervations which are responsible for the turning of the wheel, it follows from these facts *that harmonic processes of innervation occurring simultaneously affect each other in such a way that the periods of both processes are either equal or in the ratio of simple multiples of each other.* It requires great determination to withstand this law. I consider it possible that where this succeeds the deviation from the law is only apparent, not real. In reality it might be possible that one of the two harmonic processes was stopped temporarily. The facts, however, suffice to show that two harmonic processes of innervation for different parts of the body, occurring simultaneously, influence each other and are most liable to form processes of equal period.

The same is true not only for two or more simultaneous processes of motor innervation, but also for simultaneous sensory processes and motor innervations, as is proved by dancing. The rhythm of the music and the period of the motor innervations of the legs and body coincide.

3. A priori it would follow from these facts that two simultaneous *aperiodic* processes will in general interfere with or inhibit each other. That this is to a certain extent true is shown by the experience that we cannot do two things well at the same time. We

must add, however, the provision that the two things are aperiodic. If they be periodic, the opposite is true. We cannot solve an equation while jumping over a broad ditch. According to Fechner's interpretation of this fact the brain at any time has only a certain amount of energy at its disposal. In jumping over a ditch all the energy is supposed to pass into the muscles and nothing is left for the process of thinking. I showed fourteen years ago that Fechner's conception was not correct. The inhibition of a process of thought by simultaneous muscular activity is greater when we innervate one arm than when we innervate both arms simultaneously. According to Fechner, however, the greater the number of muscle-groups that were innervated the more energy must be consumed in the brain. In these experiments I measured the maximal pressure which the flexors of the hand are able to exert on a dynamometer. This pressure does not decrease when the other hand or all the muscles are innervated simultaneously, but even increases (3). The further application of this method explained the fact that we cannot well be mentally and physically active at the same time.

If we begin by solving a moderately difficult problem in mental number work, and if we attempt when in the midst of the task to attain the highest dynamometrical pressure with the hand, the pressure remains from 20–30% below the maximum that we otherwise attain when we devote our attention to the pressure alone (3, 4).   It often occurs, however, that the maximal pressure is obtained while reckoning. In this case the experimenter certainly interrupted his reckoning while pressing.   This is shown by the fact that in this case either the task is not solved correctly or the problem is entirely forgotten by the subject experimented upon.   It was a great exception if the maximal pressure was attained and the task also solved correctly.   The experiments result quite differently, however, when the experimenter first begins by pressing, and the problem is given when the maximal pressure has already been reached, so that it is only necessary to keep up the pressure. In this case I noticed no, or only a very slight, influence of both activities : the person could reckon correctly, although with effort, and the curve either did not descend, or descended but little lower than without the reckoning.

Thus we see that a simultaneous, static innervation, no matter how strong, does not prevent the reckoning ; that, on the other hand, a rapidly increasing maximal motor innervation disturbs the process of reckoning perceptibly.   I have attempted to discover whether a sudden stoppage of motor innervation—that is, a sudden relaxation of the statically contracted muscles—disturbs the process of reckoning.   This is not the case.

Whatever may be the explanation of these phenomena, we see that two simultaneous, maximal, aperiodic processes of innervation which require an effort disturb each other. *On the other hand, if they have not a maximal intensity they can take place simultaneously. I found that easy tasks or the reproduction of simple matters of memory did not lower the maximum of the pressure.*

4. These experiments recall the disturbances of associative memory which were discussed in the preceding chapter. By causing powerful processes of motor innervation to go on, we interfere with all associations, except those which have occurred very frequently. This was the characteristic of the patients mentioned in the preceding chapter. But at the same time it does not exhaust the case. The processes of innervation in the brain of these patients were possibly mutilated not only in intensity but also in other dimensions or directions.

Perhaps the cases of the inhibition of reflexes also belong in this same category of phenomena. We have mentioned that a dog with severed spinal cord shows pendulum-movements of the hind-legs when they are allowed to hang down. But if we press the skin of the tail gently the pendulum-movements of the legs at once cease (Goltz). Some authors seem to be under the impression that a shock-effect must consist in the exhaustion of the parts under the influence of the shock. This is not necessarily true. The shock-effect may be due to a phenomenon of interference or to a comparatively slight physical change which results in a mutilation of the processes of innervation.

The rôle which the intensity plays in the case of two simultaneous processes of innervation recalls the influence two simultaneous wave-motions have upon each other. A superposition of two waves is only possible as long as the amplitude is not too great. It looks as if two processes can occur simultaneously in our brain only when their intensity is weak enough to allow a superposition.

It is perhaps allowable to pursue this possible analogy of the processes of innervation with wave-motions a step farther and apply it to the process of association. A process remains associated with those processes in our brain which occur quite or almost simultaneously. Let us imagine that every process in our central nervous system has a definite form in so far as it can be represented by a curve in which the time-elements are represented by the abscissas and the intensity of the processes by the ordinates. If two processes take place simultaneously and their intensity is not too strong, they superpose each other. The traces which this process leaves in our central nervous system correspond to the curve which is determined by the superposition of both elementary curves. If one of the processes takes place later on, the other process also is reproduced by resonance. On the other hand, a very complicated process may reproduce simpler processes, which are contained in the former as constituents and have already occurred once before in their simple form. Our experience concerning sound-sensations shows indeed that simultaneous simple harmonic motions may in our sensations fuse to a compound sound of definite character (*Klangfarbe*). Moreover, a trained ear is able to decompose a compound *Klang* into its simple harmonic constituents. The mechanism of associative memory must share these peculiarities of our organs for the perception of sounds. I believe that what we commonly call intelligence depends partly upon the development of this power of resonance of the mechanism of association.

The existence of phenomena of resonance in our nervous processes may account for the fact that stimulation of the same organ yields entirely different results if we change the character or rhythm of stimulation. Only certain sounds cause a dog to howl; only a certain way of rubbing the skin of a frog causes the animal to croak. The so-called law of the specific energy of the sense-organs has pushed these important facts into the background and has tried to convey the idea that the character of the stimulation was something indifferent. Although it is true that a blow on the eye gives rise to a sensation of light, nobody would for one instant mistake this light-sensation for one caused by ether-vibrations. It is of course impossible to throw light on this subject from the anatomy or histology of the brain. But our experiences in regard to sound-sensations promise the possibility of an analysis of these phenomena. Hermann and Mach come to the conclusion that the physical resonance-theory of Helmholtz is no longer tenable, and that it may have to be substituted by a physiological resonance-theory (6, 7). According to Hermann, we may assume that the nervous end-organs themselves are especially sensitive for stimuli of a definite period (7). A generalisation of this assumption would lead to an understanding of the above-mentioned fact. The motor organs of the larynx may be considered as resonators, and this would explain why only certain tones cause a dog to howl and why only friction of a certain character — *i. e.*, periods — causes a frog to croak. The fact of the easy transmission of sounds into innervations to the larynx in human beings and parrots or song-birds would depend on the same principle. But in theories of this character we must leave some leeway for the influence of chemical processes. The phenomena of correlation which we notice in many animals during the period of heat may be determined by substances circulating in the blood during that period (internal secretion). This may account for the change in the irritability during that period.

5. Our space-sensations are varieties of three dimensions. The main coördinates show a definite relation to the main axes of our body. This leads us to a consideration of the possibility whether certain structural conditions of our body determine the main coördinates of our system of space-sensations. Hering has shown that the motor innervations of our eyes may be reduced to three kinds, corresponding to the

main axes of our body : (1) innervations to move our eyes from right to left, or *vice versa ;* (2) innervations to move them up and down ; and (3) move them from a near to a far object, or *vice versa* (8). The first motion takes place along the transverse axis, the second along the longitudinal, and the third along the dorso-ventral axis. The experiments on the horizontal semicircular canals of the ear show that the stimulation of this canal produces motions of the eyes, head, or even of the whole animal in the plane of this canal. Our experiments on galvanotropism indicate the existence of a simple relation between the orientation of certain motor elements in the central nervous system and the direction of the motions produced by their activity. This is supported to a certain extent by the experiments on the crura cerebelli. It thus seems possible that simple geometrical relations of structure are responsible for the fact that all our innervations may be reduced to three classes determined by the main axes of our body. On the other hand, Mach furnished the proof that the will or the process of innervation for a motion is of the same character as the process of space-sensations (5, 6). The will to move our eyes to a certain point and the space-sensation itself can be added algebraically. The experiences derived from space illusions caused by imperfect motility of the eyes or hands agree with this view. Moreover, Mach has proved that we recognise the geometrical symmetry of two figures very easily only when the axis of symmetry coincides with that of our body (5, 6). All these facts indicate that the main coördinates of the physiological space are determined by structural peculiarities of our body. The ultimate structural elements in this case are not necessarily of a morphological or histological order. They may be, as Mach has intimated in another connection, the stereochemical configuration of certain molecules (1). As it is not my intention to enter here upon a discussion of the nature of the space-sensations, but to indicate what place they may occupy in a future mechanics of the activity of the brain, these hints may suffice.

BIBLIOGRAPHY.

1. MACH, E. *Die Principien der Wärmelehre*, p. 360. Leipzig, 1896.

2. LOEB, J. *Zur Theorie der physiologischen Licht- und Schwerkraft-Wirkungen. Pflüger's Archiv*, Bd. lxvi., 1897.

3. LOEB, J. *Muskelthätigkeit als Maass psychischer Thätigkeit. Pflüger's Archiv*, Bd. xxxix., 1886.

4. WELCH, J. C. *On the Measurement of Mental Activity through Muscular Activity*, etc. *The American Journal of Physiology*, vol. i., 1898.

5. MACH, E. *Contributions to the Analysis of the Sensations.* Chicago, 1897.

6. MACH, E. *Die Analyse der Empfindungen und das Verhältniss des Physischen zum Psychischen.* Jena, 1900.

7. HERMANN, L. *Beiträge zur Lehre von der Klangwahrnehmung. Pflüger's Archiv*, Bd. lvi., 1894.

8. HERING, E. *Die Lehre vom binocularen Sehen.* Leipzig, 1868.

INDEX

CLASSICS IN PSYCHOLOGY

AN ARNO PRESS COLLECTION

Angell, James Rowland. **Psychology:** On Introductory Study of the Structure and Function of Human Consciousness. 4th edition. 1908

Bain, Alexander. **Mental Science.** 1868

Baldwin, James Mark. **Social and Ethical Interpretations in Mental Development.** 2nd edition. 1899

Bechterev, Vladimir Michailovitch. **General Principles of Human Reflexology.** [1932]

Binet, Alfred and Th[éodore] Simon. **The Development of Intelligence in Children.** 1916

Bogardus, Emory S. **Fundamentals of Social Psychology.** 1924

Buytendijk, F. J. J. **The Mind of the Dog.** 1936

Ebbinghaus, Hermann. **Psychology: An Elementary Text-Book.** 1908

Goddard, Henry Herbert. **The Kallikak Family.** 1931

Hobhouse, L[eonard] T. **Mind in Evolution.** 1915

Holt, Edwin B. **The Concept of Consciousness.** 1914

Külpe, Oswald. **Outlines of Psychology.** 1895

Ladd-Franklin, Christine. **Colour and Colour Theories.** 1929

Lectures Delivered at the 20th Anniversary Celebration of Clark University. (Reprinted from *The American Journal of Psychology*, Vol. 21, Nos. 2 and 3). 1910

Lipps, Theodor. **Psychological Studies.** 2nd edition. 1926

Loeb, Jacques. **Comparative Physiology of the Brain and Comparative Psychology.** 1900

Lotze, Hermann. **Outlines of Psychology.** [1885]

McDougall, William. **The Group Mind.** 2nd edition. 1920

Meier, Norman C., editor. **Studies in the Psychology of Art: Volume III.** 1939

Morgan, C. Lloyd. **Habit and Instinct.** 1896

Münsterberg, Hugo. **Psychology and Industrial Efficiency.** 1913

Murchison, Carl, editor. **Psychologies of 1930.** 1930

Piéron, Henri. **Thought and the Brain.** 1927

Pillsbury, W[alter] B[owers]. **Attention.** 1908

[Poffenberger, A. T., editor]. **James McKeen Cattell:** Man of Science. 1947

Preyer, W[illiam] **The Mind of the Child:** Parts I and II. 1890/1889

The Psychology of Skill: Three Studies. 1973

Reymert, Martin L., editor. **Feelings and Emotions:** The Wittenberg Symposium. 1928

Ribot, Th[éodule Armand]. **Essay on the Creative Imagination.** 1906

Roback, A[braham] A[aron]. **The Psychology of Character.** 1927

I. M. Sechenov: Biographical Sketch and Essays. (Reprinted from *Selected Works* by I. Sechenov). 1935

Sherrington, Charles. **The Integrative Action of the Nervous System.** 2nd edition. 1947

Spearman, C[harles]. **The Nature of 'Intelligence' and the Principles of Cognition.** 1923

Thorndike, Edward L. **Education:** A First Book. 1912

Thorndike, Edward L., E. O. Bregman, M. V. Cobb, et al. **The Measurement of Intelligence.** [1927]

Titchener, Edward Bradford. **Lectures on the Elementary Psychology of Feeling and Attention.** 1908

Titchener, Edward Bradford. **Lectures on the Experimental Psychology of the Thought-Processes.** 1909

Washburn, Margaret Floy. **Movement and Mental Imagery.** 1916

Whipple, Guy Montrose. **Manual of Mental and Physical Tests:** Parts I and II. 2nd edition. 1914/1915

Woodworth, Robert Sessions. **Dynamic Psychology.** 1918

Wundt, Wilhelm. **An Introduction to Psychology.** 1912

Yerkes, Robert M. **The Dancing Mouse** and **The Mind of a Gorilla.** 1907/1926